This book is dedicated to
my Aunt Maysel;
my second mother, my
spiritual mentor, and
the person who taught me
to pray.

I wish to thank my wife, Cathy Brady, my daughter, Marian Brady, and my best friend, Bob Wallace for proof-reading and supporting me in the writing of this book.

Contents

Introduction

This book is the second book in my series, Life in the Spirit. It is all about prayer. This book will make sense to you without having read my first book, The Holy Spirit – Life in the Spirit.   However, without a proper understanding of the Holy Spirit and who He is, you will find this book impotent. I encourage you to read The Holy Spirit – Life in the Spirit, before you delve into this one.

This book is very different from any other book you have ever read about prayer. Because of this, I would like to ask you to take everything you know about prayer and put it in storage for awhile. Try to read this book without any preconceived ideas about prayer. Start from scratch and you will see prayer in a whole new light.

We have an amazing God! He created the heavens and the earth. He created life. He parted the Red Sea and the Jordan River. He provided food and water to 2 million people in the desert for 40 years. He delivered Shadrach, Meshach and Abednego from the fiery furnace and He delivered Daniel from the lion's den. He brought bones back to life. He healed the sick, gave sight to the blind, walked on water and raised the dead. He is the author of Grace.

We have lost sight of this God when we pray. Our prayers are not to the God who created the heavens and the earth. Our prayers are to a little God; sometimes a teeny tiny God. A God who can do nothing unless it is according to His mysterious will. We pray to a God who is weak and powerless; a God who is fickle and capricious, a God who is limited by time, space, circumstances, attitudes, money, power and popularity. We pray to a God who used to work miracles; but, no longer does so. In fact, we no longer PRAY to God at all: We make wishes to God like tossing pennies into a wishing fountain.

I felt led by the Holy Spirit to write this book on prayer. This is a book that teaches and encourages Christians to pray to a big God, to know and fellowship with Him, to ask for big things and to develop an intimacy with Him in a new way. Christians should anticipate our God to provide all of the resources, time, money, talent, and opportunities necessary for us to accomplish His will in our lives.   We stifle and limit God in our lives because we think so very small.

How I Write

I love to write; especially writing about the Lord. I feel a great sense of responsibility when I write. It is my objective to make sure that the things that I am writing about are true and consistent with God's word. I also feel the need to assist people in their walk with God.   I don't see myself as a spiritual superior. I see myself more as the guy passing out cups of water to runners in a marathon race. Most of the time, I am learning right along with my readers. It is often times like I am reading someone else's book.

Anytime that I am writing about spiritual things for public consumption, I follow a three-fold path as I write.

1. I spend time in prayer before each writing session. I ask the Lord to fill me with the Holy Spirit and to lead me into truth as others read the words that I have written. I also ask the Lord to open my Readers heart to His truth.
2. As the Holy Spirit guides me, I seek confirmation from Pastors and Teachers who are learned and wise for what I hear from the Holy Spirit. I listen to their sermons and read their writings. I don't seek out confirmation; but, I listen to whatever they are currently teaching. Out of nowhere, they will confirm what I have just written; even if the sermon is about something completely different.
3. I do not write unless I sense the presence of the Holy Spirit.

Who This Book Is For

This book was written for Bible believing Christians who are seeking a closer relationship with God through prayer. It was written for those Christians who would like to experience a new intimacy and strength with God, who would like to be effective in their prayers, and would like to learn to pray with boldness and power.

> *"You will seek me and find me when you seek me with all of your heart."*
> *Jeremiah 29:13 NIV*

Chapter 1: Prayer and Salvation

It would seem logical that one would begin a book on prayer with a chapter titled "What is Prayer?". I must confess that I started out to do just that in the writing of this book. Then the Holy Spirit prompted me to start the book looking at prayer from a different direction; looking at prayer in conjunction with salvation.

The number one question most asked to Pastors is the question, "*How can I be sure that I am saved?*' Salvation is a certainty; there should never be any doubt.   The New Legalism, doing things for Christ in our own strength and power, creates doubt in the minds of Believers. It creates a dichotomy: Jesus is our Savior but we need to do works to keep or earn our salvation. The idea of "*Are we doing enough for Jesus?*' is weaved throughout the dogma of the modern church. It is constantly being taught to us through our devotions, through our small groups and through our sermons. The result is that we have doubts about our salvation. Doubting our salvation is one of Satan's most purulent attacks against Believers.

The fact is this is the number one question asked of Pastors is evidence that a great deal of the preaching and teaching in the church today is a works-based theology. The Bible is very clear that *Jesus is the way, the truth and the life* (John 14:6), *that whoever believes on him shall have everlasting life* (John 3:16*), that unless a man is born again he cannot see the kingdom of God* (John 3:3). Very simple. Very easy. Yet many Christians are still wondering whether or not they are going to heaven?

 Accepting Jesus as our personal Savior is all that is required; however, before we can accept Jesus as our Savior we need to recognize that we need to be saved and what we need to be saved from. Only the Holy Spirit can make us aware of this. Simply mouthing the words will not make us a child of God.   These words accompanied by a life-altering- change in and of the heart and initiated and mentored by the Holy Spirit, is the confirmation of salvation.

> *The sacrifice that you desire is a broken spirit. You will not reject a broken and repentant heart, O God.*
> *Psalm 51:17 NLT*

If we accepted Jesus because we wanted to go to heaven, or because we were afraid of going to hell, or because someone convinced us intellectually that we should follow Jesus, then we may not know God at all. <u>Prayer is not possible without salvation so if we are finding prayer dull and ineffective it may be because we do not have a relationship with God.</u>

Only the blood of Jesus Christ will enable us to enter into His presence (Heb. 4:16). Only the blood of Jesus Christ can cause our own spirit to be reborn and it is in and through our newly born spirit that we are able to know and communicate with the LORD God Almighty (John 4:24).

Prayer (fellowship with God) begins at the moment of salvation. The Holy Spirit convicts us of our sin. We have not seen God but, by the power of the Holy Spirit, we come face-to-face with a glimpse of His presence. Like Isaiah coming into the presence of God for the first time, we should feel this:

> *Then I said, "It's all over! I am doomed, for I am a sinful man. I have filthy lips, and I live among a people with filthy lips. Yet I have seen the King, the LORD of Heaven's Armies."*
> *Isaiah 6:5 NLT*

The holiness of God. Who can stand in His presence without being completely consumed? Who can see God and live? (Ex. 33:20).

It is at that moment that our own spirit is born and we come alive in Christ. It is at that moment that we begin a relationship with the Author, Designer, Architect, and Creator of the universe.

It may be that your moment of salvation was dramatic and filled with emotion. It may be that your moment of salvation was peaceful and bliss. It does not matter. Either way or anything in between, the quintessential attribute of salvation is a life-altering-change in the way that we think, feel, and act. We are no longer plugged into the realm of flesh and desire but into the realm of holiness. Flesh and desire are still present; but, our own spirit has become alive and is hungry for the things of the Spirit. The Holy Spirit will begin to change us and slowly we become more like Jesus. The more we yield to the Holy Spirit, the faster that change will be.

Additionally, the fundamental characteristic of this life-altering-transformation is the catalyst of *change*.   Are we changing because we are supposed to? Are we trying to be good Christians? Are we acting because we should? These are fine intensions but they are based in human effort and will eventually fail.

The catalyst of our transformation must be our new spirit's thirst for the holiness of God; otherwise, the change is not real. It is the nature of our born again spirit, in conjunction with the Holy Spirit, that activates holiness and the desire to be holy within us.

Which is more real: A husband who gives his wife a present on her birthday because he is supposed to OR a husband who gives his wife a present on her birthday because she is dear and precious to him and he wishes to show it?   The first husband is acting out of duty, obligation, method. Love may or may not be involved. The second husband is acting out of the heart. His love for his wife generates the nature of giving within him; within his heart. God sees our heart.

You cannot hide your heart. Jesus said:

The holiness of God must come from our hearts; not our minds. The holiness of God must come from our nature; not our intellect. Only the Holy Spirit can generate holiness within our nature. Only by yielding to the power of the Holy Spirit can our nature take on the attributes of holiness.

It is from this nature, from this heart, from this holiness (made possible by the blood of Jesus Christ and mentored by the Holy Spirit) that we can enter into the very presence of God (Heb. 4:16) with our hopes, fears, worries, joys, praise, excitement, disappointments, petitions, love, complaints, anger, etc.

It is this new hunger for holiness that instills in us the desire to commune and fellowship with the Source of all holiness: God. Communion and fellowship with the Source of holiness is prayer. If we are not praying, then we are not in communion and fellowship with holiness. We are not yielding to the Holy Spirit. We are not empowered. We are not growing spiritually. We are living life in our own strength and our own power. We are living life alone!

The Story of the Two Wolves

There is a old story that has been used on dozens of TV dramas about 2 wolves (sometimes it is told as two dogs). Some attribute the original story to the Cherokee. It goes something like this: Inside all of us is a battle between two wolves. One is evil; full of anger, regret, bitterness, ego, lies, lust, greed, self pity, and pride. It is filled with worldliness. The other wolf is good (holy); full of joy, love, peace, compassion, truth, mercy, faith and kindness. It is filled with the Spirit. The one that you feed is the one that wins the battle.

Prayer is feeding the good wolf. Sometimes we get caught up in worldliness. We all do it. No one is immune because we are still creatures of flesh and blood (the bad wolf) living in a fallen world. The more we live in and pay attention to the world, the more we feed the bad wolf and the good wolf goes without food. Sooner or later, the good wolf begins to die of starvation.

As I stated in my first book in this series, "The Holy Spirit - Life in the Spirit":

> **Prayer is so vital to our Christian walk and our life in the Spirit that unless we are spending a good deal of time in prayer every day, we will not have much of a relationship with God at all!**

Reading the word of God is important and useful for teaching, rebuking, correcting and training in righteousness (2 Tim. 3:16). Fellowshipping with other Believers is essential to our spiritual growth (Heb. 10:24-25). <u>Yet none of these is more important than or even equal to the value of prayer!</u>

Prayer is simply not possible without salvation. Without salvation, the spirit is dead. We can only communicate with God through our spirit.

It is therefore necessary to ask yourself, "Am I truly saved?" Have I asked Jesus to be my Savior? Have I experienced that life-altering-transformation initiated by the Holy Spirit? Have I come before the Lord with a broken spirit; a broken and contrite heart?

If you have, then move on! Never spend any more time doubting your salvation! If you haven't, now is the time.

Open your heart to God. Listen to the Holy Spirit. He will lead you in the way that you should go and your prayer life will begin for the first time.

Chapter 2: The Will of God

Another reason that many Christians have difficulty with unanswered prayer is that they do not understand the will of God. There is a lot of confusion about the will of God. Much of this confusion is the result of misunderstandings and false beliefs. This leads to some really weak prayers. I would like to share my understanding about the will of God so that you might have a different perspective.

A great many Christians believe that the will of God is unknowable. This was often true in the Old Testament (except for the Prophets and certain select people). While the Old Testament is still true, in the New Testament, our standing with God is very different. In the New Testament, we have a relationship with God (Rev. 3:20) that did not exist in the Old Testament because of what Jesus did for us. We also have the Holy Spirit to guide us into all truth and in and through our sanctification process; being more like Jesus (I Peter 1:2).   <u>Because we can talk with God and God can talk with us, the will of God is not something that should be elusive and unknowable for us</u>.

The more we yield to the Holy Spirit through prayer and reading the word of God, the more we know the will of God (Rom. 12:1-2). We **can** know God's will for our lives. You can't pray for 3 minutes a couple of times a week and know the will of God. The more time we spend in prayer and reading the word of God, the more in tune we become to God's will in our lives.

Let's look at how to know the will of God. First, we need to visualize the will of God a little differently.

Journey Versus Destination

Many Christians spend their lives focused on the destination: Heaven. We go to church, we give tithes and offerings, we help the poor, we pray before we eat a meal, we have devotions every day all so that when we die, we will go to Heaven. Unfortunately, none of this will get us into Heaven. Only through repentance brought on by the Holy Spirit and accepting Jesus Christ as our personal Savior can we go to Heaven.

Once this happens, our lives are no longer about the destination. The destination is known. It cannot be obtained because you already possess it (Rev. 21:2-7). It is sealed by the Holy Spirit (Ephesians 1:13). It cannot be earned. It cannot be lost or stolen. It is assured. It is guaranteed. It is promised. (John 14:2-3)

Once we have become a child of God, our spiritual life in the body is no longer about the destination; <u>it is now all about the journey</u>! The journey is our walk with God here on earth and the mission He has planned for us. It is about the here and now. The destination of Heaven is guaranteed and promised to the Believer. The journey, the here and now, is neither guaranteed nor promised. We need to focus. We need to focus on walking in the Spirit and doing the thing(s) that God has called us to do in the here and now. Too many of us; especially older people, spend their time on earth focused on the destination completely ignoring the mission God has for them in the here and now.

It is now about the journey; otherwise, we would all be whooshed off to heaven after we accepted Jesus Christ as our personal Savior. We remain here because there is a purpose to our presence. We remain here because there is a purpose to our salvation; more than just getting into Heaven. We remain here so that we can be utilized by God in the service of His Kingdom and His Plan. We remain here so that we might have fellowship with Him; the Author, Designer, Architect, and Creator the Universe (1 John

1:3). We remain here as an example to unbelievers as the flavor and the light of life (Matt. 5:13-16). We remain here to help the poor, the fatherless, the sick and those in need (Prov. 22:9).

It is this fellowship, this intimacy, this relationship with God that draws us into prayer. It is this fellowship that reveals the will of God to our spirit. A Christian who does not spend quality time in fellowship, on a daily basis, with the Father in prayer is going through life blind and alone.   Without spending time in prayer, it is impossible to know the will of God.

Like A River

A great many Christians believe that the will of God is a fixed, very narrow path that God has designed only for them. This combined with the belief that the will of God is unknowable puts a lot of Christians in a constant state of turmoil seeking the will of God in their lives and making corrections for having missed the narrow path. As a result, their spiritual and physical lives are spent either in limbo waiting on God or in correction to get back on the narrow path.

These Christians who think that the will of God is narrow and fixed like a train track are never accomplishing anything for God. They remain in a constant state of seeking God's will: This is the job God wants you to have, this is the spouse God wants you to marry, this is the home God wants you to live in, this is the car God wants you to drive, and so on. They are afraid they will make a wrong decision because *once you get off track, it is very hard to get back on track!* Nothing could be further from the truth!

Think of the will of God like a mighty river; like the Amazon, the Mississippi, or the Nile. It is broad and deep. We are in the river (the will of God). Within the river there are many choices. While we are in the river, we can move freely within the river boundaries. We have the freedom to move to any point in the river. Whatever position that we chose, we will still be in the river (we will still be in the will of God). We can dive down deep, we can move to the slow current areas, we can move to the fast current areas, we can take a break on an island; we are still in the river.

Occasionally, we get out of the river to check out the scenery. When we do, we get out of the will of God. God, through the Holy Spirit, eventually or perhaps suddenly will coax us back into the river where we can continue our journey. The point being that if we have strayed away from the will of God, either through sin or misguided thinking, all we have to do is to jump back into the river.

Sometimes the river goes over a waterfall or through a cave. When this happens, everyone in the river must go through it because it is the only choice possible. There are no other choices. There is only one direction, one choice, one outcome. However, the river is, most of the time, gentle, broad, and fluid.

God's will is like that. Sometimes the job you take, the person you marry, the house you live in and other choices are important or integral to the plan God has for your life. In these cases, God will make His will known. He will give you clear direction.

At other times God simply wants you to choose and trust Him that He will guide you.

The Marriage Example

Marriage is a very good example. Most people spend a great deal of time and worry as to whether or not the person they are marring is "the right person for me" or "the person God wants me to marry." When they do marry and troubles enter into the marriage (which they inevitably do), their first response is that they chose the wrong person to marry. They got off the narrow track of God's will and now they are hopelessly doomed to spend the rest of their life married to the wrong person! A very small God indeed! He is able to speak the universe with its systems, cycles, and beauty into existence; but, He is unable to mold and change you and your spouse into something wonderful, precious, and holy?

Many, many people believe that marriage is a treasure chest; a box containing all sorts of good and wonderful things. They believe that when you marry *the right person*, you will both receive many wonderful benefits, so choosing the right mate determines the bounty of your box. You and your spouse will visit the treasure chest each day and take wonderful and precious things from its bounty. If you choose the right mate, your life will be wonderful. This just is not true!

The truth is that marriage is an empty box. There is nothing in the box except a bunch of feelings. Feelings come and go so the box really has no value whatsoever. For your marriage to work, you and your spouse must visit the box regularly and fill it will treasures. Those treasures are children, grandchildren, arguments, sickness, the death of friends and loved ones, money problems, health problems, vacations, weddings, picnics, etc. The empty box gets filled with the precious things that your marriage created, experienced and endured. At the end of life, the once empty, worthless box is now filled with treasures far too valuable to be measured or counted.

Regardless of how good looking your husband is or how beautiful your wife is, these qualities have nothing to do with a successful marriage. A successful marriage is based solely upon your commitment to the marriage and your commitment to the Lord; nothing else! The choice of whom you marry is not nearly as important as the commitment that you've both made to the marriage and to the Lord. Marriage is hard work regardless of who you marry.

God may bring a potential mate into your life or perhaps several potential mates. If you are feeling led by God to get married, pray to Him and ask Him for guidance and direction in selecting a mate. Believe that God will guide you. Provided you are both Christians and you have similar goals, attractions, and beliefs, God will bless any decision that you make. If the person you choose is simply the wrong choice for you or if it is not the right time, God will intervene and put a stop to the union because you have put your trust in Him to guide and direct you!

Don't waste your energy trying to find that one person that God has for you. It is highly unlikely that this is God's plan. Marriage is constructed from the ground up based upon a mutual attraction. It is not a move-in-ready structure.

Rather than focusing on the question, "Is this the right person for me?", focus on the question, "Do we have the level of commitment necessary to make this work?"

It is important to note that all choices have consequences. The choice you make will produce a different outcome from another choice. Remember that before God placed the first star in the sky, He knew what choice you would make so don't get so hung up on making the right choice.

The most important thing of all is to remember that the river (God's will) is going to continue to flow whether we are in the river or not. God's will is going to take place regardless of where we have decided to be within the river or outside the river. Our involvement is simply for our benefit; but, our involvement or lack of it will not affect the flow of the river in the least. God does not need our involvement to make the river flow. God wants us to enter the river so that we might be blessed. God also wants us to enter the river because He desires fellowship with us (James 4:5).

Be In Motion

Sometimes we are faced with choices that appear equally to be the right thing. We want to make the choice that God wants us to make so we spend time in prayer and perhaps get others involved in the praying. We then wait to hear from God usually doing nothing in the process. This is the opposite of faith:

Sometimes God wants us to wait (Ps. 46:10). Sometimes God wants us to simply make a choice and then trust Him enough that He will be sovereign over the situation <u>even if we made a bad choice</u>. God cannot steer a parked car. The car must be in motion. We must be in motion in order for God to guide us. We cannot be holed up in some cave somewhere seeking the will of God nor hiding out in our living rooms. We must be in motion! Then God will respond to our faith bringing to us the people, the circumstances, the resources, and the opportunities necessary to fulfill His plan for our lives. If we are in the will of God, we even have immortality until we have fulfilled God's purpose for our life.

<u>Prayer, the Word of God, and the Holy Spirit combined with faith (motion) will reveal the will of God to us clearly and succinctly</u>. It sometimes doesn't happen overnight; but, often times God responds immediately to our faith.

Don't be afraid to make choices; especially, don't be afraid that you will make a bad choice because, at some point, you will. Don't be afraid because God is looking at your heart and He knows that you are trying to please Him. He knows that you love Him. He knows that you want to do the right thing. God created everything. He is certainly willing and able to lead you in the right direction even if you are going the wrong way.

Let me be clear here, we are talking about Christians making choices that involve trusting God. We are not talking about sin choices. The consequences of sin is death (Rom. 6:23). Also, we reap what we sow (Gal. 6:7). Christians who are seeking to please God through their choices can be rest assured that God's blessing will remain upon them and that God is sovereign in ALL circumstances (Romans 8:28).

Christians sometimes make foolish choices and we do stupid things. We sometimes trust the wrong people. We sometimes confuse our own desires for the will of God. We sometimes fail our spouses or our children. Yet, we can find comfort in knowing that God is sovereign over every circumstance and that He is able to steer us through the choices we have made; foolish, stupid, or otherwise.

Knowing that God's will is not some mysterious, unknowable jewel that is extracted from religious ceremony and discipline.   God's will becomes clear to us through <u>prayer, the Word of God, and the Holy Spirit combined with faith (action)</u>. Knowing God's will is a critical component of answered prayer.

Chapter 3: Answered Prayer

To understand answered prayer, we should begin with the characteristics of prayers that get answered. Here's a list. There are probably more.

Characteristics of Prayers That Get Answered

Reverence

Approach

Confidence

Persistence

Humility

Compassion

Gratitude

Reverence

God responds to our reverence for Him.

> *While Jesus was here on earth, he offered prayers and pleadings, with a loud cry and tears, to the one who could rescue him from death. And God heard his prayers because of his deep reverence for God.*
> *Hebrews 5:7 NLT*

Jesus is the Son of God; yet, the book of Hebrews says that God heard His prayers because of His reverence for God, not because of His standing or status. We too should possess this deep reverence for God; especially during our prayers.

The book of Proverbs tells us that fear (reverence) of the LORD is the beginning of wisdom (Pr. 9:10). Proverbs also says that fear (reverence) of the LORD is the beginning of knowledge (Pr. 1:7).

The first 4 of the 10 commandments deal with honoring and revering God. This is very important to Him. When Israel worshipped idols, God described the act as adultery (Ez. 23:37)! By calling idolatry adultery, this illustrates how God sees His relationship with us.

Remember that the primary reason we are here is bring glory to God (Isaiah 43:7). Our prayers and our prayer requests should bring glory and honor to God.

Approach

The Bible is full of teachings, promises, and examples about prayer and about praying effectively. Yet, it remains one of the most misunderstood and illusive conventions in our walk with God. We very often turn prayer into a religious procedure or a religious method. Jesus taught us to think of God as our Father (Matt. 6:9). It is almost entertaining to hear some people pray in public. They even get a different voice when they pray; almost machine-like. They also develop a rhythm that is almost poetic. Listen to your prayers. Is this the way you would talk to your earthly father?

Our Father in heaven loves us far more than our earthly fathers. What's more, our Heavenly Father is perfect in His responses (Matt. 7:11), knows us better, knows the exact condition of our lives, and knows what we have need before we ask Him (Matt. 6:34). He knows our strengths and weaknesses (Heb. 4:13). Our approach to Him should be nothing short of the way we would approach our own father. The writer of the book of Hebrews said it best:

The blood of Jesus Christ has cleansed us so perfectly that we can enter into the very presence of God our Father without fear of judgment.   This is an awesome privilege. It is perfectly fine to enter into His presence fully clothed in our humanity and weakness. That is, it is okay to go before Him and cry like a baby, to beg and plead, even to be angry and question His thinking. This is part of the processes of brokenness; of surrendering our problem or circumstances to our Father. Our broken heart is God's broken heart.

The story of Jesus raising Lazarus from the dead (John 11:1-44) gives us great insight into how God relates to our pain and trouble. Verse 35 says, "Jesus wept." The person who let Lazarus die so that He could raise him from the dead, wept. The person who knew that Lazarus would be alive again in just a few minutes, wept. Jesus (God), because He loves us so very much, so connected with our suffering that He suffered with us; even though He knew the outcome would be the total restoration of the life of Lazarus.

Confidence

Confidence embraces the ideas of faith, certainty, and assurance. God responds to our confidence in Him.

If your Aunt Betty tells you that she is coming to stay with you for a couple of days, do you wait for her to arrive to make preparations? No. You believe she is going to arrive;

therefore, you change the sheets in the guest room, buy extra food, get out the good dishes, etc. You go into action before you see any evidence of her arrival. This is faith in motion (action): believing without evidence (Hebrews 11:1).

This simple principal is one of the key components of answered prayer!

It is lack of faith (confidence in God), or more specifically, unbelief, that causes many Christians to have unanswered prayers and pray for very small things. I am not talking about the Matthew 17:20 verse about moving mountains; I am talking about the sabotage that most Christians bring into their prayers: *if it be the will of God* from 1 John 5:14.

> *This is the confidence we have in approaching God: that if we ask*
> *anything according to his will, he hears us.*
> *I John 5:14 NIV*

The New Testament talks about prayer a great deal including direct teaching and examples from the life of our Lord Himself. Jesus teaches us about prayer in all four gospels both by word and by example. He teaches us how to pray. He teaches us that the relationship that we have with God is that of a father to his children and that God loves us with an endless love.

We are taught over and over again, by the Lord Jesus Himself, that whatever we ask for in prayer we will receive. The only "conditions" are an active relationship with God (salvation, walking in the Spirit, and prayer) and belief that God is able (faith). Every teaching in the New Testament teaches this. Yet, a whole army of Christians default to 1 John 5:14 as a "condition" of prayer. They say that our prayer must be *the will of God.* We do not know the will of God; therefore, it is impossible for us to pray with any kind of confidence (faith) at all! Without confidence, how can we be filled with anything but doubt that God will answer our prayer?

We get caught up in the "will of God". Because we think we cannot know the will of God we pray with doubt (the very thing that James warns will result in unanswered prayer). Of course our prayers need to be the will of God; but, the will of God is not elusive and unknowable. If we are walking in the Spirit we have access to the will of God (Rom. 12:1-2). If we are not walking in the Spirit, our prayers become cries of hope rather than cries of confidence. <u>Without confidence (faith) that He will hear our prayers and answer our prayers, our prayers are nothing more than hope.</u>

These Christians who constantly default to the unknowable will of God (I call them "Willers") are praying prayers that contain virtually no faith at all. They are actually anti-faith. Every Bible-believing church has them. They are usually one of the pillars of that church; pastor, elder, deacon or trustee. They express glee at the prospect that God might not answer this prayer because His will is unknowable. They are joyful and triumphant when God doesn't answer a prayer. The truth is that so much doubt is created by Willers, with their unknowable will of God mantra, that no one believes God will answer the prayer. Pillars of the church or not, they are emissaries of Satan bringing doubt and weakness to prayer. They are toxic to prayer and toxic to the church. I've seen whole churches full of them.

<u>We must believe that God will answer our prayer; otherwise, He will not!</u> Yielding to some unknowable, enigmatic "will of God" is anti-faith. It is guaranteed unanswered prayer. It is why so many Believers have an ineffective prayer life, pray for very small things, and have a very small God.

> *And without faith it is impossible to please God, because anyone who comes to him must believe that he exists and that he rewards those who earnestly seek him.*
> *Hebrews 11:6 NIV*

We learned in the last chapter that God's will **IS** knowable to those who sincerely follow Him. Part of God's will is that we ask Him! The will of God is that we go to Him in prayer and ask Him. God answers every prayer. Let me say that again:

God answers every prayer!

If you have an active, personal relationship with God, He answers <u>every</u> prayer in one of four ways*:

1. **Yes**
2. **Wait**
3. **I have something better for you**
4. **No**

(* This is an adaptation that came from the teachings of Dr. Charles Stanley)

God's answer of *No* is, or should be, a rare event. God answers our prayer with *No* only when we ask for things with the wrong motives, to satisfy the desires of the flesh (James 4:3), ask for things that are against God's design, or ask for things not believing that He will provide them. God answers our prayers with "No" because we did not consult with Him before we asked.

Praying with confidence means that we pray expecting God to answer; not hoping that God will answer. Knowing that God answers every prayer should give us a new dimension to our prayer life and our spiritual growth. We should be motivated to spend more quality time with God so that we may know His will in our lives and to know what to pray for. We should go boldly before God and ask God to do amazing things because we know His will and because we are completely confident that He will answer our prayers.

Persistence

In Matthew 7:7, the words Ask, seek, and knock in the original Greek indicate ongoing and persistent. Matthew 7:7 and the parable of the Persistent Friend (Luke 11:5-13), is Jesus teaching us that <u>one of the keys to answered prayer is persistence</u>.

Many of our prayers go unanswered simply because we give up praying. Often times God has to prepare the circumstances, prepare the hearts, or prepare the conditions for the prayer to be answered. Sometimes He needs to prepare us. Sometimes it can take years. Never give up. Never stop praying.

My Grandfather prayed that my Mother would come to know Jesus. He prayed this consistently for years and years. He told me that God has promised him that he would see my Mother in heaven. My Grandfather never saw my Mother come to Lord. He passed away without ever seeing his prayer answered. About 10 years after his death, my Mother accepted the Lord Jesus as her personal Savior. She became an incredible woman of God and my Grandfather's prayers were answered. She led many people to Christ and influenced the lives of many, many Believers. God had to work on her heart and her circumstances until she had no choice but see Jesus as the only way, the only truth and the only way to life. It took a very long time.

My grandfather never gave up. He was faithful in beating on God's door every day. Did he get discouraged? I am sure that he did from time-to-time; but, he remained persistence and, in the end, God gave him the desire of his heart.

Humility

Humility embraces the ideas of being humble and modest. God responds to humility.

> *And he gives grace generously. As the Scriptures say, "God opposes*
> *the proud but gives grace to the humble."*
> *James 4:6 NLT*

I once heard a sermon on humility where the Pastor stated that humility is one of those things that if you think you have it; you don't. If you think you don't have it; you do.

Over and over again throughout Scripture we can see that God hates pride and arrogance (Prov. 16:6). One of the trademarks of this current world is that we have become a prideful and arrogant generation in all our ways. We have become insolent, disrespectful, contemptuous, inconsiderate, self-absorbed, and self-centered. We have become all the wickedness and evil listed in Romans 1. What's more, we are proud of who we are and confident that we can make a new and better world. Somehow we miss the fact that with every new generation we become more wicked and depraved.

As Christians, we have to recognize that we are all sinners, that none of us are worthy to save ourselves, and that only through the blood of Jesus Christ can we enter into the presence of God. The moment we think that we have earned or deserve anything from God is the moment that our prayers become ineffective.

It gets worse. There is an underlying ideology in politics, in science, and in the Green Movement that suggests that man can fix the world. We can certainly make improvements to our world. We can certainly affect people's lives in a positive way. Also, we can certainly do things to protect and reduce our impact on the environment; however, we can NEVER "fix the world". This is pride! It suggests that we do not need God in our lives. It suggests that mankind has the power to become God. This is right out of Satan's playbook.

We have to be careful because pride is deeply ingrained in our culture and we are constantly being bombarded with propaganda about pride. It is part of our collective psyche. It is in our music, in our schools, in our cartoons on TV, in political speeches and even in some of our sermons. We may be prideful and not even be aware of it.

God hates pride (Job 22:29). To stand in the presence of God with any type of egotism or self-righteousness, at all, is certain failure when it comes to prayer.

> *Then he said, "Don't be afraid, Daniel. Since the first day you began to pray for understanding and to humble yourself before your God, your request has been heard in heaven. I have come in answer to your prayer.*
> *Daniel 10:12 NLT*

God responds to humility. We see it over and over again in the Bible. King Hezekiah (Is. 38), King David (2 Sam. 12), Parable of the Pharisee and the Tax Collector (Luke

18), and Jesus washing the Disciples feet (John 13). The Bible says that Moses was the most humble man in the land (Num. 12:3). Jesus was the epitome of humility:

Compassion

Compassion embraces the ideas of love, empathy, and kindness. God responds to compassion.

One of the characteristics of Jesus' mission is His compassion for others. The whole reason Jesus died on the cross was because of His compassion for the world (John 3:16). God answers prayers rooted in compassion.

I generally detest prayer meetings and group prayers. For one thing, one can never hear what half the people are praying for because they talk so softly. Additionally, the prayers are generally liturgical in nature being more form than substance. Finally, prayer meetings pray from a list and not from a prompting of the Holy Spirit. God puts certain events and people on our hearts and these are the things we should be praying for. I am often asked to pray for my neighbor's brother's cousin's uncle who is dying of cancer or looking for a job. Unless the Holy Spirit puts this on my heart, I feel no compassion or empathy for this person. Without compassion or empathy, my prayer will not be effective. I simply don't pray for it.

God lays different things on our hearts. God gives all of us different jobs, different gifts, different circumstances and God lays different things on our hearts. There are people who have a deep compassion for the homeless. Others have a deep compassion for single mothers. Others have a deep compassion for foreign missions. Others have a deep compassion for those caught in sex trafficking. The list goes on and on. God gives us different things to pray for. He gives us different things to support and encourage. He gives us different assignments. It is simply not possible to have compassion or empathy for every single problem on the planet.

Don't pray for something unless you are prompted by the Holy Spirit to do so. Don't allow the devil to poke you with guilt because you have no empathy for a certain good cause. Satan wants you to be praying for everything because it will keep you distracted so that you cannot focus on the assignments that God placed in your heart.

On the other hand, I was in a group prayer once when a man was asking for prayer for his friend. His friend had an operation that did not go well. The man was left paralyzed from the neck down. The doctors told him he would never walk again. When I heard this, I felt something move inside of me for this man's condition. For some reason, the Holy Spirit filled me with compassion for this man and his family. The Holy Spirit reached out to me and told me to pray for this man. I did. I continued to pray for him both publicly and privately. Six months later, against all the knowledge and predictions of the doctors, the man was standing upright and walking. Praise be to God in heaven!

Prayer meetings convey the idea that every Christian should be praying for every problem that exists in the world. This just isn't the case. If the Holy Spirit doesn't "connect" you to the problem or the event, then there is no compassion. <u>Without compassion, the prayer is just words</u>.

Gratitude

Gratitude encompasses the ideas of thankfulness, appreciation, and gratefulness. God responds to gratitude.

> *The one who offers thanksgiving as his sacrifice glorifies me; to one*
> *who orders his way rightly I will show the salvation of God!"*
> *Psalm 50:23 ESV*

I think that gratitude is one of the most powerful forces in the universe. It is seconded only by love.

For many years I suffered from severe depression. Many, many days I was suicidal. I prayed and asked God to deliver me from this affliction and I heard Him say just one word: Gratitude! The Holy Spirit taught me that depression was nothing more than self-pity with an engine; self-pity on Red Bull. Self-pity is sin. My self-pity was fueled by my being ungrateful for everything in my life. The Holy Spirit led me to take charge of my depression, empowering me to do so, and I began to thank God for every single thing in my life; no matter how big or how small. Pencils, paperclips, electricity, my car, my house…everything!

Very quickly, within minutes, the depression was gone. It would come back the next day or perhaps even the same day. I would repeat the process. This actually went on for over a year; but, with each episode, my depression was getting less and less. The hopelessness and despair of depression lost its grip on my life; day-by-day, moment-by-moment, depression was defeated.   Finally, after years of struggle, without medication or professional help, I walked away from depression. Gratitude was the reason. It is very powerful.

Gratitude and its cousin, Thanksgiving, are extolled to us again and again in the scriptures; in both the Old and New Testaments (Ps. 50:23, Col.3:17, 1 Tim. 2:1).

> And give thanks for everything to God the Father in the name of our Lord Jesus Christ.
> Ephesians 5:20 NLT

> Be thankful in all circumstances, for this is God's will for you who belong to Christ Jesus.
> 1 Thessalonians 5:18 NLT

These are some of the commonalities to answered prayer, or more specifically, to effective prayer. By effective prayer, I mean that we are praying boldly, knowing what to pray for, asking God for big things, expecting God to do those things, and seeing God answer those prayers over and over again.

The more time we spend in fellowship with God through prayer, the more these "qualities of answered prayer" become a natural part of our prayer universe.

Chapter 4: Developing Prayer Skills

Many Christians lack, what I call, prayer skills. Most of us don't think of prayer as a skill; but, praying effectively and with significance is a skill. It is a skill that can be learned.

We pray all kinds of strange things, executed in strange ways, based upon strange beliefs taught to us by people of God who also learned to pray that way. In effect, the vast majority of Christians are still praying the way we learned to pray when we were 5 years old.

> Brothers and sisters, I could not address you as people who live by the Spirit but as people who are still worldly—mere infants in Christ. I gave you milk, not solid food, for you were not yet ready for it. Indeed, you are still not ready. You are still worldly. For since there is jealousy and quarreling among you, are you not worldly? Are you not acting like mere humans?
> 1 Corinthians 3:1-3 NIV

Here's a good way to test yourself to see if you need to develop better prayer skills. Pray a prayer, publicly or privately; however, during the prayer, you are not allowed to ask God to "bless" anybody, "be with" anybody, or pray for any medical condition. Are you still able to pray?

If the answer is that you are having a hard time or that you can't pray at all, then this is a sign that you need to develop some prayer skills.

James says:
> ...You do not have because you do not ask God.
> James 4:2b NIV

If you are praying to God, <u>be specific</u>, just like you would with your own father. When we pray "Bless Joe", what does that mean exactly? We are asking God to give Joe good (undefined and indeterminate) things. Is that something that can be witnessed? Is it something that we can look back and say, "God answered this prayer?" No! The prayer is far too vague. How do you give glory to God when you have prayed for vagueness? How do you tell that something actually happened? Instead of asking God to "Bless Joe", let's ask God to do something more specific for Joe. <u>Let's pray for something where we can see God working in Joe's life and we can see God answering our prayer.</u> Then we can all come together and share what God did in Joe's life with others and God can then be glorified through our prayer. Additionally, our faith and our understanding of how God works in our lives will grow.

The same thing is true when we pray "Be with Joe." What does that mean? If Joe is a Christian, God is always with him? We should instead pray that God provide him with peace through this difficult time, or God give skill and insight to the doctors as he goes through this procedure, or God protect him as he travels to Tallahassee.   Ask God to give or do something specific.

 If Joe is not a Christian, then we should pray that God use this difficult time to open his eyes to Jesus. Bottom line: let us pray in such a way that we can see God answering or working on our prayer request. "Be with Joe" is just a useless, empty prayer.

Unskilled prayer simply takes a prayer request and then applies a default, measureless prayer to the request!

A lot of our prayers go unanswered because our request is so vague and ambiguous that it is impossible to know whether or not the prayer was answered.

It should also be noted that there are times when it is perfectly acceptable to ask God to "be with" someone or to "bless" someone. Sometimes we don't know what to pray for and our prayer has to be generic and vague. The point is that the generic and vague prayer should never become our standard, default prayer. It should be our rare, occasional prayer.

A strong focus on Medical prayers can be another tell tale sign of needing to develop prayer skills. Now, first I should say, there is nothing wrong with praying medical prayers. Medical prayers are an essential part of our prayer life. We should all be active in praying for the specific healing of others. For many people; however, medical prayers are the only form of prayer that they know how to pray. In most prayer meetings, a great deal of the time is spent discussing and praying for medical problems. The prayers are simple and generic and never really ask God for a specific outcome. Very little time is spent in discussion about how we might pray so that God may be glorified or that others may believe through this situation. No time is spent in seeking the guidance of Holy Spirit.

Since most of our prayers are so broad and general that answers to our prayers cannot be determined, we spend little or no time in prayer meetings discussing how God has answered our prayers! If God is God, and He is, then our prayer meetings should be full of amazing stories of how God has answered our prayers and worked in our lives. Our prayer meetings are just the opposite. They are solemn. Very often it seems like public prayer and prayer meetings descend into a collection of formularies for the glory and satisfaction of those who are present with God being just a prop.

We are praying to God, a consuming fire (Deut. 4:24), yet our prayers treat Him almost as if He does not exist. We are praying to God, the Creator of all things (Gen. 1:1), yet our prayers treat Him as a wimpy God who can do only very small things. We are praying to God who loves us so much that He sent His only Son into the world to die for our salvation (John 3:16), yet in our prayers we totally ignore fellowship and worship with Him. We are praying to God, who understands our pain and suffering (Isaiah 53:4), yet our prayers treat Him as one who is dispassionate to our circumstances.

If you want to pray with skill, then pray to a God who is able to do immeasurably more than we can ask or imagine (Eph. 3:20), go boldly into His presence in fellowship (Heb. 4:16), and don't worry about anything, pray about everything, tell God what you need and thank Him for everything He has done (Phil. 4:6). Pray to a God who knows what you have need of before you even ask (Matt. 6:8).

Get rid of the default prayers that ask God for broad, generic things and pray for specific things. He is your Father, your very dear and precious Father. You are His child, His very dear and precious child. Have the same relationship with Him that you would want your children to have with you. Expect God to hear you and to answer your prayer; not in some distant future but now…today!

Preparing To Pray

We can pray anywhere at any time. We can pray standing, sitting, laying, upside down, underwater, on our knees, in a car, on a boat, or in an airplane. Buzz Aldrin prayed on the moon. There is nothing wrong or unholy about any of this.

There is, however, a need for a special daily prayer in our spiritual walk. Jesus rose early in the morning (while it was still dark) and slipped away to a solitary place to pray (Mark 1:35). Effective prayer requires us to have a solitary place where we can be alone with God without interruption. We should also try to set aside the same time each day.

Personally, I like to get up about 3:00 am, make a cup of coffee and sit in the dark talking to my Father. This is my way. I'm not suggesting that it be yours. You do, however, need to have a private place to pray. If you are not doing this already, you will soon find that this is the most beneficial thing you can do every day. Communicating with the Source of all things on a daily basis will bring a centered focus to your life that is difficult to explain.

If you honor God and honor your relationship with Him by setting aside time in a solitary place with Him, He will reward you immensely. He will give you insight, wisdom, clarity, and understanding about all the situations in your life. You will understand His will for your life and understand how to pray and what to pray for.

Stirring the Pot

It could be that there is a situation in your life or in the life of someone that you are praying for that has remained in a state of limbo or status quo for months or years. It could be a horrible job, an addiction, an unequally yoked marriage. It doesn't get any better and doesn't get any worse.

When we begin to pray for this situation using our new found prayer skills, we are effectively stirring the pot. God will begin to bring about the circumstances, events, conditions, brokenness, etc., to answer this prayer. The situation will no longer be in a state of status quo but in a state of change. <u>Usually the change will seemingly be for the worse!</u> This should be a key indicator for us that God is working in this situation; that God is answering our prayer. The situation has remained stalled for many years and now it is changing: this is God!

Change, in any situation that we have been praying for, is always evidence that God is working to answer your prayer. Even if the change is making the situation worse, this is

God bringing about the conditions necessary to answer your prayer. The proper response is praise and thanksgiving.

There was a fellow in my Bible study who was having trouble with his boss at work. It seems his boss was using fowl language and did not like the fact that this fellow was a Christian. The situation had been in a state of limbo for a while; getting no better or worse.

Our Bible study began to pray for this situation and God began to intervene. At first, the boss increased his attacks. Then the company was sold to another company. The nice stable job that our friend had was now riddled with uncertainties. Our friend was so unsettled that he requested prayer to calm the situation down; effectively asking for the return of everything to the way it was. I reminded him that we were praying for change and it was change that we were getting. We needed to let God work this out.

The uncertainty continued for several more months. Our friend lost some of his perks. The shop was not doing so well so his income was starting to decrease. In his eyes, It seemed that God had abandoned him.

Finally, another job opportunity came up. He interviewed for the job and got it. The job paid more money, had a better work environment, had better benefits, better hours, and had a better long term outlook. It took almost 2 years from the time we started praying to the time that God fully answered the prayer. It took a long time because my Bible study friend had a very hard time trusting God. God took him to the breaking point; not only to ultimately bless him, but also to teach him to believe in the power of prayer. This story is classic. It illustrates how God works in our prayers.

Praying In The Name of Jesus

John, moreso than the other gospels, teaches us to revere and respect the name of Jesus. The name of Jesus is powerful! Used by a person filled with the Spirit of God, it can wipe out the power and influence of demons and demonic activity in a person's life, it can heal, and it can bring calm to overwhelming situations. We, being good 5 year olds, have interpreted this to mean "magic words" and so, we end all our prayers with the magic phrase, "In the name of Jesus we pray. Amen."

This is ludicrous. We pray in the name of Jesus by living the lifestyle that He wants us to live; not by adding magic words to end of our prayers! The Sons of Sceva (Acts 19:13-16) thought the name of Jesus was a magic word and used it as such to cast out demons. This resulted in the demons attacking them.

Praying in the name of Jesus is a lifestyle not a method or formula. James illustrates this by noting that Elijah was an ordinary man who, because of his lifestyle, prayed that it would not rain and it did not rain for 3-1/2 years (James 5:17).

Our prayers are not answered because we added the magic words to end of our prayers. By accepting the shed blood of Jesus as our righteousness, He brings our own spirit to life. Our prayers are answered because we are the children of the LORD God

Almighty. We are precious to Him. By walking in the Spirit, He reveals His will to us, He hears our prayers and He answers them.

Glory To God

The most fundamental aspect of effective prayer is that God is glorified. When we pray broad, vague prayers that have no quantifiable outcome, there is no way to know whether or not God answered the prayer and, most important, God is not glorified in our prayer.

As I pointed out in my first book, glorifying God is our primary purpose. 40% of the 10 commandments dictate God's requirement for our loyalty, honor, reverence, and respect. Jesus repeatedly addressed this in His teachings:

> *Let your light so shine before men, that they may see your good works*
> *and glorify your Father in heaven.*
> *Matthew 5:16 NKJV*

Paul did as well:

> *May the God who gives endurance and encouragement give you the*
> *same attitude of mind toward each other that Christ Jesus had, so that*
> *with one mind and one voice you may glorify the God and Father of our*
> *Lord Jesus Christ.*
> *Romans 15:5-6 NIV*

One of the primary reasons that God answers prayer is so that He might be glorified (John 14:13)! <u>One of the primary ingredients of skilled prayer is praying in such a way that God will be glorified</u>. How do you do that? Here are some examples:

- A public prayer or a prayer meeting where skilled prayer contenders pray earnestly for a specific outcome. God answers the prayer and the whole group rejoices and praises God.

- A private prayer where a prayer warrior prays earnestly for a specific outcome. God answers the prayer. The prayer warrior then takes the answered prayer to the public as a testimony. People hear the news of what God has done and rejoice and praise God.

- A private or public prayer where the skilled prayer contenders pray earnestly for a specific outcome in a limbo situation. When God brings change into the stalled situation, even though He has not yet answered the prayer, He makes His presence known by bringing about change. Praise God and glorify Him.

<u>God sometimes answers prayers made in secret; however, this is not an effective prayer strategy</u>. Even if you tell others after the fact, the praise and worship is not as meaningful as having included others from the beginning. Avoid secret prayers. Involve others; but, make sure they are not Willers.

In a public prayer session where there are a bunch of Willers present during prayer request time, I simply keep my requests quiet. The Willers will sabotage any power that the corporate prayer might have by injecting doubt into the corporate prayer.

Of course, the broad, vague prayers bring no glory to God at all. No one ever knows if the prayer was answered because nothing was ever actually asked!

Fasting

Fasting and prayer go together like peace and joy or mercy and grace. It is difficult to have one without the other. I talked about fasting in the first book of this series, "The Holy Spirit – Life in the Spirit" (available on Amazon), so I will just cover the basics in this book.

The Bible time and again talks about fasting; however, the Bible does not really explain fasting. It just assumes you know all about it. To add to the confusion, the role of fasting in the New Testament is different from its' role in the Old Testament.

Old Testament fasting was different from New Testament fasting because we have the blood of Jesus Christ who restored our fellowship with God (Col. 1:20-22) and the Holy Spirit working in us (2 Cor. 3:18). Old Testament fasting included fasting as means of mourning (II Samuel 1:12), as an appeal to God for mercy (Esther 4:16), as a component of repentance (Joel 2:12), as a component of petitioning the LORD (Daniel 9:3-19), and to humble themselves before God (Ezra 8:21). As Christians, we have salvation through Jesus Christ our Lord and, because of His mercy and grace, we can go directly into the presence of the Father with our mourning, our appeal for mercy, our repentance, and our petitions. God, through Jesus Christ, replaced religious procedure with fellowship with God (Gal. 3:23-26); we became the children of God (1 John 3:1).

We are all composed of two selves: (1) the carnal self concerned with the physical realm; and (2) the spiritual self (dead in unbelievers) concerned with the spiritual realm. Fasting denies the carnal self and focuses our attention on the spiritual realm.

Fasting is simply humbling ourselves before God (Ezra 8:21) and denying our fleshy nature so that the awareness of our spiritual nature is elevated. We communicate with God through our spirit because He is Spirit (John 4:24). We fast because it elevates our spirit; gives more dominance to our spiritual nature. As a result, we are able to commune with God more effectively (Rom. 8:26), see His will in our lives more clearly, and worship Him more fully (Dan. 9). There is nothing holy or magic about fasting. It is simply drawing nearer to God so that He will draw nearer to you. It is mostly humbling ourselves before Him, surrendering ourselves to Him, and fellowshipping with Him in a way that is different from our daily walk with Him.

Fasting is not a spiritual requirement. There will be plenty of people in heaven who have never fasted. However, if you need to draw near to God for special understanding of a situation or special clarity to a situation, fasting is one of the best ways to do this. At the end of a fast, you should have experienced a new balance in your life. You should have some degree of clarity and understanding that you did not have before the fast. Often times, fasting simply slows down the focus of your life enough to allow the Lord to lay everything out for you so that you understand. You may not walk away from a fast with all the details; but, you will certainly walk away with a view of the situation from a mountaintop.

In 2019, I was diagnosed with lung cancer. In prayer and fasting I sought out fellowship with our Father to understand why this was happening. Within minutes of starting the prayer and fasting, the Lord spoke to me and assured me that I would be healed. I did not know the details, but I knew the outcome. Additionally, He gave me the peace that passes all understanding. I never once prayed that I would be healed because the Lord had already promised me that I would be healed. I lost no sleep over this matter at all.

My wife, Cathy, on the other hand, was a mess in the beginning, as any wife or husband would be in that situation. She would actually get angry with me because I was so calm. When I explained to her the understanding that had been given to me from the Lord, she understood and then received that same peace from God. From that moment forward, we went through the 6 month process with perfect joy and peace.

We had many people come to us to provide comfort and support. We very much appreciated the prayers and love that was poured out on both of us; however, it was difficult for them to understand our peace or the promise that was given to me. I think they might get it now.

I started out with stage 3 lung cancer. The plan was to remove one lobe of my lung (we have 5 lobes) and then 4 months of chemotherapy and perhaps radiation. The pathology from after my surgery revealed stage 1.6b instead of stage 3. Additionally, my doctors all agreed that chemotherapy and radiation was unnecessary! Today I am cancer-free with virtually no health limitations. <u>God delivered on His promise that was given to me during prayer and fasting.</u>

Return To Aunt Betty

Let's return to the trip that Aunt Betty is planning to make to our house. Let's look at the way we might pray for her as she makes this trip. We used to pray this:

> **Lord, be with Aunt Betty as she makes this trip to my house. I ask that you will keep her safe and show her traveling mercies. Bless the time that we will have together. Amen.**

This is a nice innocent prayer that basically asks God for nothing! Now that you are learning to have prayer skills, let's pray this instead:

> **Father, I thank you and praise you that you have created this special time with Aunt Betty and me. I ask that you will provide time and opportunity for us to enjoy each other's company. I ask that she will sleep well while she is here and that she will be comfortable with her room. I ask that you will keep her car in good working order as she makes the trip to and from my house. I ask that you will keep her from getting into an accident. Keep her awake and alert for the whole trip.**

Let her meet good Christian people along the way to make her trip smooth. Amen.

If you were Aunt Betty, which prayer would you prefer to be prayed for you?

The second prayer is specific. It addresses specific things that we can look back and point to how God answered this prayer. We can praise Him from this prayer. God can be glorified from this prayer. As a matter of fact, half of this prayer will be answered the moment that Aunt Betty arrives at the door. You can thank and praise God the moment of her arrival!

The more time we spend in prayer, reading the word of God, and listening to the Holy Spirit, the more we will be in tune with the will of God. The more we will know what to pray for.

Form Versus Function

I want to be careful here not to lead you down a path of procedure and method for prayer because that is never going to bring glory to God either. We have a relationship with our spouse, with our children, with our friends and with our co-workers. These relationships are enhanced when we bring certain attributes and qualities to our relationships; love, consideration, respect, etc.

We learned these attributes from others as we were growing up. If we learned badly, such as throwing temper tantrums, we need to unlearn this behavior, at some point, if we are to have a normal relationship with other people.

The same is true with our relationship with God. We learned to pray badly when we were very young and never advanced into a more mature manner of talking to God.

This means that our relationship with God is juvenile. A great many Christians have a dysfunctional relationship with God because of it. We need to unlearn the dysfunctional way of praying. We need to develop a deep, personal, intimate relationship with our precious Heavenly Father.

If we put things into perspective, God has put us here to fulfill His plan for our lives. God does not call any of us to do mediocre things for Him. He has provided us with access to the people, opportunities, resources, finances, and events necessary to accomplish His purpose for our lives. Having a truly functional prayer life is one of the keys to accessing His plan and the tools He has provided for us to do extraordinary things for the Kingdom of God.

Don't Play God

We are the children of God and loved by God (1 John 1:3). We are also servants of God (2 Cor. 6:4). We have a tremendous power in prayer: As Christians, we can walk into the very presence of God knowing that we are loved as His dear children and ask Him for anything.

Let us not ask out of greed or pleasure. Let us tune in to the holiness of God. Let us partake of His righteousness. Let us understand the plan of God for our lives so that we know what to pray to for. Before we go around praying for things, let us seek first to understand His perspective, His plan, His thoughts. Let us understand His will; especially His will for our own lives.

Chapter 5: The Nature of Prayer

Every year there is an online auction to have a private dinner with billionaire, Warren Buffet. It is a charity auction for the Glide Foundation of San Francisco. In 2019, the winning bidder paid a little over $4.5M dollars for the privilege. Warren Buffet is the darling of Wall Street and investors everywhere because he has amassed so much wealth during his lifetime. In reality, Warren Buffet is a simple man who used a tried and true method of investing called "Value Investing" and became very, very good at it. He certainly should be respected and admired. He certainly has some wisdom and some knowledge; but, I'm not sure that his insight would be worth $4.5M for an 1 hour of his time; but, it's all for charity, right?

Being a Christian is like having dinner with a very important person. This VIP; however, just happens to be the Author, Designer, Architect, and Creator of all things! We not only have access to Him for dinner, but we also have access to Him for breakfast, lunch, snack, work, bedtime, and everything in between. On top of that, He loves us very much and He can't wait to enjoy our company. Can you image the value of such a thing. As Believers, we have such a thing. We didn't have to bid anything. Jesus Christ paid our way on the cross and now we have unlimited access to the Father.

> *Because of Christ and our faith in him, we can now come boldly and confidently into God's presence.*
> *Ephesians 3:12 NLT*

James says that God longs for our fellowship:
> *Or do you think Scripture says without reason that he jealously longs for the spirit he has caused to dwell in us?*
> *James 4:5: NIV*

Very few Believers take advantage of the fellowship opportunities we have with the Father. Most of our prayers are quick and obligatory as before a meal or during a church service. What a waste of the most powerful, the most precious endowment that God has made available to Believers. A great price was paid to give us this privilege. The benefits are abundant. Instead, we waste it on doing things in our own wisdom, in our own strength, and in our own way.

Prayer is nothing more than spending quality time with our Heavenly Father. Prayer, much like reading the Bible, gives us access to holiness and wisdom for our lives. Prayer enables us to know the will of God; especially the will of God for our own lives. It is important, in fact, I would say it is the most important activity that we can do as Christians.

The Types of Prayer

The types of prayer differ depending upon who is doing the talking. One of the reasons for this is that there is overlap in prayer types. I have selected 8 different types of prayer for this book:

THE 8 TYPES OF PRAYER

Daily Surrender
Fellowship
Worship and Praise
Thanksgiving Prayer
Praying For Others
Petition/Supplication
Healing
Spiritual Warfare

There is also the prayer of repentance which is not listed as the prayer of repentance is a onetime event. Our relationship with God begins with the prayer of repentance. Repentance is initiated by the Holy Spirit and is very different from the other types of prayer. The prayer of repentance introduces us to God and His Kingdom. The other prayers are privileges that only the children of God may access.

Other than the Prayer of Daily Surrender, the 8 types of prayer are simply guiding principles for your prayer journey. <u>I am not describing a method here; I am describing a landscape</u>. Please don't write this list down and then pray from the list; you would be missing the whole point of this book. There is no order to the prayer types. Your prayer can include all or some of the prayer types.

We will look at each of these types of prayer in detail. One chapter of this book has been dedicated to each of them.

Praying in the Spirit

Some people define *Praying in the Spirit* as a prayer type. It is not. Paul says:

> *And pray in the Spirit on all occasions with all kinds of prayers and requests. With this in mind, be alert and always keep on praying for all the Lord's people.*
> *Ephesians 6:18 NIV*

Praying in the Spirit is a way to pray in any type of prayer. Praying in the Spirit happens when we are praying to the Father and words simply do not express our joy, our pain, our grief, our empathy, our thanksgiving or our compassion for a situation. Our spirit simply communicates raw emotion directly through the Holy Spirit (Rom. 8:26).

Many Christians have never prayed in the Spirit because it seems unstructured and unordered. Many Christians have prayed in the Spirit and did not know it. From the verse in Ephesians (6:18), we see that Paul encourages us and recommends that we pray in the Spirit. It is part of putting on the full armor of God (Eph. 6:10-18).

Jude also tells us to pray in the Spirit as a fundamental attribute of waiting for the return of our Lord Jesus Christ:

> *But you, dear friends, by building yourselves up in your most holy faith and praying in the Holy Spirit, keep yourselves in God's love as you wait for the mercy of our Lord Jesus Christ to bring you to eternal life.*
> *Jude 1:20-21 NIV*

To pray in the Spirit, simply let go. As you are praying to the Father and emotions begin to well up inside of you, simply let go. Let those raw emotions flow directly through your prayer; without words.   Let the floodgates of your heart open and pour out its contents in the presence of our Creator. It may or may not be accompanied by speaking in tongues; not the languages of people here on earth, but in the language of the angels (1 Cor. 13:1).

> *For if you have the ability to speak in tongues, you will be talking only to God, since people won't be able to understand you. You will be speaking by the power of the Spirit, but it will all be mysterious.*
> *I Corinthians 14:2 NLT*

It may be accompanied by crying, laughing, or moaning. Praying in the Spirit produces within us a sense of balance; a centered approach to life. It is far more than the peace that passes all understanding (Phil. 4:7). It is a spiritual grounding.   It is more analogous to the glowing face of Moses after he spoke with the LORD (Exodus 34:29-35), than to the peace that passes all understanding (Phil.4:7). While we don't have radiant faces, we have an inner radiance that can be seen by others in our outer appearance.

The Lord's Prayer

I've attended many sermons and Bible studies that used the Lord's Prayer as a basis or outline for prayer. There are whole books on prayer that do so as well. While these sermons, Bible studies, and books are all very interesting; perhaps even useful in learning to pray, the Lord's Prayer is not the quintessential guide to prayer that many of us make it out to be.

The Disciples asked the Lord Jesus to teach them to pray the same way that John the Baptist taught his disciples to pray (Luke 11:1). We don't have a description of the prayer that John the Baptist taught his disciples; but, we do know what Jesus taught His disciples. Jesus gave them what is now known as the Lord's Prayer (Matt. 6:9-11).

The Lord's prayer is a very special prayer because it is an *interim prayer* just as John the Baptist's prayer was an interim prayer. It introduced us to idea of a personal God whom we addressed as Father. The prayer taught the disciples to pray, but this was before the lamb of God was sacrificed and rose again on the 3rd day. It was taught before the Holy Spirit was given. It was taught before we could enter into the presence of God washed clean by the blood of Christ. The disciples, before the death of Jesus, were still sacrificing animals to cover their sin.

Jesus could not teach His disciples to pray, before the cross, the same way they would pray after the cross. While there is nothing wrong with praying the Lord's prayer, it is not the iconic method of prayer that we make it out to be. Jesus Christ has given us direct access to the Father, the forgiveness of all sin, and the Holy Spirit to guide us into all truth. Jesus never prayed in the Lord's Prayer format. There is no record of Peter,

Paul, James, and John having used the Lord's Prayer format in their prayers in the Epistles or teaching it to others. The reason is because it is an interim prayer meant to serve the disciples of Jesus until the death and resurrection of the Lamb of God.

The Lord's Prayer contains the phase, "thy kingdom come". Jesus said:

> *But if it is by the Spirit of God that I drive out demons, then the kingdom of God has come upon you.*
> *Matthew 12:28 NIV*

When Jesus died on the cross, rose again, and the Holy Spirit was given at Pentecost, the kingdom of God (the realm of God) came. The interim period of Jesus was over.

Corporate Prayer

Corporate prayer is simply praying as a group or collective; prayer meetings and public prayers are common examples. This can be an extremely effective way to pray; however, as I have previously indicated, I am not a big fan of most corporate prayer because it often diverges into gossip, praying to a small God, and defaulting to the unknowable will of God.   It turns into a collection of Christians who simply hope that God will do something!

When the opposite is true: Believers coming together with genuine concern, believing in a powerful God who is able to answer prayers, and who walk in the Spirit of God and are able to discern the will of God, then corporate prayer becomes powerful. It is exciting because we are part of a collection of Christians who know that God is working!

Then there is the often miss applied Matthew 18:20:

> *For where two or three gather in my name, there am I with them.*

Matthew 18:20 NIV

This is often quoted and prayed in the context of corporate prayer. <u>Verses 15-19 are given by Jesus in the context of corporate discipline, not corporate prayer</u>. It is given for how church leaders are to deal with the authority of Christ; in this instance, dealing with a member of the congregation who is actively sinning. The meaning and context of the verse is that Jesus, and His authority and blessing, is with the two or three church leaders from the church who are doing the disciplining (or exercising the authority of Jesus in some other capacity).

The antithesis of the misapplied Matthew 18:20 would mean that wherever two or three are not gathered in His name that He is not there with them. We know that this is not true!

Proper corporate prayer is very powerful. It is a good way to not only get things done but also to build the faith of the congregation; especially the faith of the weaker members. When God is answering prayers and getting things done, faith grows. This is how it was in the early church. The early church was very effective at spreading the gospel because it was comprised of Christians who actually believed that God answered prayer. God was answering their prayers! God was answering their prayers because they believed God was answering prayers!

I don't see this very often in corporate prayer today. I don't see God doing big things in our churches because no one believes in this type of God anymore. In today's church our prayers consist of "wishful thinking prayers" and "wishful hoping prayers". This is very sad because our Lord and Savior paid such a high price to reconnect us to God and to empower us with the Holy Spirit.

Mature Christians should be asking God for big things! Mature Christians should be expecting God to do big things. Our prayer meetings should be full of amazing stories of how God has answered our prayers. I simply cannot believe the namby-pamby nature of our prayers to the LORD God Almighty. Let us pray to a big God who loves us and is able to do incredible things in and through us.

Chapter 6: The Prayer of Daily Surrender

The gist of my first book "The Holy Spirit – Walking in the Spirit" (available on Amazon) was to introduce you to the person of the Holy Spirit and to recognize that you can do nothing for God in your own power and strength. When we accept Jesus as our personal Savior, the Holy Spirit seals our salvation (Eph. 1:13). This is static and guaranteed. It has to do with the destination: heaven. As Christians, we also need a daily filling of the Holy Spirit (Eph. 5:18) which is different. The filling has to do with the journey; the path that God has chosen for us. The verb filling in Ephesians 5:18 indicates an on-going, daily process.

We cannot serve God without daily surrendering our will to His will. We cannot serve God without daily empting ourselves of ourselves and being filled with the Spirit of God. We cannot serve God unless we are daily strengthened and empowered by the Holy Spirit. We cannot serve God unless we are relying on the Holy Spirit to create opportunities, provide wisdom and insight, to lead us into all truth, and to provide all the resources required to accomplish and fulfill the plan that God has called us to do. This applies not only to the His long term plan for our lives, but also to the here and now of each person's daily life.

If we are trying to serve God instead of allowing God to work through us, we are not serving God!

In a sermon by Pastor Greg Groeschel, he made the comment:

> **God can do more with your surrender**
> **than you can do with your control.**

Stop trying to do things for God. Yield! Surrender! Allow God to work in and through you. Expect God to work in and through you and He will. You will find that your life will become extremely effective for Christ. You will bear much fruit (John 15:5). It will be in the form of bringing others to Christ, sharing the Good News of Christ, and responding to the needs of others (orphans, widows, prisoners, and the hungry).

Learn to respond to the Holy Spirit working in your life. Don't try to make things happen, simply respond to what is already happening. Play the hand you have been dealt. There is no random and there are no coincidences in the life of a Believer. God is working in you and in everything around you. He puts people and resources in our paths all the time. If we are expecting God to be active in our lives, we will see it. If we are not expecting God to be active in our lives, we will not.

What Does The Daily Surrender Prayer Look Like?

An example of the Daily Surrender Prayer would look like this:

> **Holy Father in heaven,**
> **I surrender my will to do your will.**
> **I surrender my goals, my ambitions, and my thoughts to you.**
> **I surrender my past, my present, and my future.**
> **I surrender my family, my income, my health, and my finances.**
> **Fill me with your Spirit.**
> **Empower and enable me to serve you today.**
> **Create opportunities for me to share the gospel, to help others, and to be a light to other people in the world.**
> **Enable me to be an example to others.**

**Enable me to hear your voice and give me the courage to do whatever it is that you ask me to do.
Amen.**

When we pray a prayer like this, God will work in our lives.

Expect God to be working in your life!

When we pray a prayer like this, everything that happens in our day will have the distinguishing marks of God branded into it. If we are expecting it, we will see it. If we are not expecting it, we will miss it.

The person in front of you at the grocery line, the person behind you in the cafeteria, the article you read on your newsfeed, the email you received from someone, the extra time you had after work, the thought you had about a new business idea, etc., everything that happens in a surrendered day has the hand of God in it.

Opportunities are usually interpreted by the church to mean opportunities to share the gospel. This may be true; however, as a Christian you are praying about a lot of things. Your God-surrendered day is probably about more than just evangelism opportunities. For example, if you've be praying for your friend Mary to find a job, expect God to answer that prayer and be aware that there is a high probability that He will answer that prayer through you…through the opportunities generated in a God-surrendered day. Perhaps you've been praying for a new car to replace your worn out car. Expect God to answer that prayer and it is highly likely that the answered prayer will come to fruition within your God-surrendered day.

We miss so many answered prayers simply because we are not expecting God to be working on the solution. We miss so many opportunities simply because we are not looking for God in our daily lives.

In a God-surrendered Christian's life, nothing is random, nothing is insignificant, and nothing is coincidence. It doesn't mean that everything is life changing, but everything contains the imprint and workings of God. Look for it! Expect it!

When things don't go as planned, we need to look for God to be involved in some way. He Is sending us on an adventure. We should embrace it. Watch and observe what is happening. If we get all stressed out, we will totally miss the opportunity that God has put in our path.

The Believer who surrenders their life to the will of God on a daily basis will recognize that trouble and/or unplanned events are almost always God at work in our lives in some way. If we are not participating in a daily surrender of our life to the plan of God, then trouble and/or unplanned events could be the work of other factors; including the works of the devil and his demon horde.

When we do things for God in our own power and strength, there is no surrender. We are not working in and through the power of God. The cause may be based in good. The intent may be based in good. Even the outcome may bring seemingly great benefit; however, this type of activity does not belong to God. It belongs to the world.

"For God to get the glory... God must fight the battle!"
Pastor Erwin Lutzer of the Moody Church in Chicago Illinois

Chapter 7: The Fellowship Prayer

<u>The fellowship prayer is undoubtedly the most important of all prayer types</u>; yet, it is probably the most neglected. Jesus rose early in the morning to pray (Mark 1:35). Sometimes Jesus would spend the whole night in prayer (Luke 6:12). Jesus is the Son of God. If the Son of God needed to spend time with His Father, then so do we.

Jesus already possessed the full measure of the Holy Spirit (John 3:34). He could heal the sick, raise the dead, produce enormous amounts of food, calm storms, walk on water, and cast out demons. What did He have to pray about? The answer is that He was fellowshipping with His Father. He was spending time in the presence of holiness and in the presence of eternity. He was spending time in the Source of all things.

I would speculate that most of us spend little time in prayer. I would also speculate that, of the time that we do spend in prayer, we spend most of that time asking for stuff. Jesus already possessed everything; yet, prayer was extremely important to Him. We need this as well.

Think back to your children again, or your parents, or your friends. The activity that generates the most amount of love and treasures is sitting together in fellowship. You're not asking for anything, they are not asking for anything, you are not complaining, they are not complaining; the simple enjoyment of each other's company. Simple fellowship with those whom you love is definitely in the top 5 best human experiences. It is the same with our Father in heaven. He enjoys fellowship with us. He earnestly longs for it and seeks it out (James 4:5).

He loves us. He is willing to grant our requests. He is willing hear our troubles. He is willing comfort our sorrows, just as you are with your family and friends. Yet, it is those times when we are intimate with each other that we learn the most about each other.

Fellowship prayer teaches us holiness and righteousness as we sit in the presence of holiness and righteousness. Fellowship prayer teaches us how God thinks and what His will is for our lives. Fellowship prayer produces godly strength within our mortal bodies. Fellowship prayer helps us to recognize the things in our lives that are really important and the things that are not. Fellowship prayer immerses us in the Source of all things.

Many Christians spend most of their prayer time praying for others and asking God to provide for things. If we had a relationship with our children, our parents, or our friends that consisted only of them asking us for things we would call this relationship dysfunctional; yet, this is the way that many Christians interact with God. In reality, most of our prayer time should be spent in fellowship. One reason is that we need the connection to the Source to empower our own lives. Another reason is that this is the example that Jesus taught.

I recognize that we live in a busy world. If we look at the ministry of Jesus, I think we would agree that He lived in a busy world as well. The crowds simply would not leave Him alone. The Scribes, Pharisees, and Sadducees were constantly trying to trap Him. The sick were always after Him to be healed. The general crowds wanted to be taught. There were so many that He had to teach from a boat (Luke 5:3). They followed Him across the Sea of Galilee (John 6:1-2). It is probably safe to say that Jesus was constantly in ministry from morning to night. Yet, our beloved Savior, needed to spend extended periods of time in fellowship with His Father, the Source.

The prayer that Jesus prayed the night before His arrest (John 17) reveals to us a great deal about Jesus and His relationship with the Father. There is a great sense of intimacy between the Father and the Son. There is love, compassion, purpose, and praise. While Jesus is asking the Father for things in His prayer, this prayer is infused with intimacy. This prayer is a Fellowship Prayer.

I firmly believe that this Fellowship Prayer is the type of prayer that God desires with His children more than any other. I believe this because this is the type of relationship that I want with my children more than any other.

Jesus introduced us to the concept of God as our Father. In doing so He was making us aware that we can have an intimate relationship with God. This simply was not possible before Jesus died on the cross. It is clear that Enoch, Abraham, Moses, King David, Daniel, and the Prophets had a very special relationship with God; however, our relationship with God is even more intimate because we can enter into His presence. Their relationship with God was one of loving reverence and obedience. Our relationship with God is one of love, mercy and grace. Our relationship with God is one of being His children.

Essential to the idea of fellowship is that the communication is not one way. We are communicating with God and He is communicating with us. It is during the fellowship prayer that God speaks to us, probably not in an audible voice, but in thoughts, ideas, and remembrances. Listen! Don't dismiss what you are hearing. God is speaking to you!

Learn to hear God speaking to you. Generally, I make a cup of coffee and sit in my prayer space talking and listening to God. It can take a little time to learn to distinguish the voice of God from the other voices in your head; but, it is relatively easy learn to hear His voice. If we take the time to do this and develop this, I promise our relationship with God will change and so will our lives.

Journaling is a good way to learn to separate the voice of God from the other voices in our heads. As the Spirit speaks to you, write these things down. Research what you write down using scripture, sermons, and conversations with friends. <u>If the message is from God, we will receive independent confirmation from one of those sources: scripture, sermons, or conversations with friends</u>. It will not take long for us to learn to know the difference. In time, we will not only hear God's voice during Fellowship Prayer, but we will also hear His voice at all times of the day. The Holy Spirit will prompt us and nudge us to say or do a certain thing. If we yield and follow this guidance, we will be amazed at the interactions and miracles that will follow.

Be aware that without the independent confirmation, it is not from God. Additionally, God does not contradict His word. God does not reveal a new doctrine or a new church-wide announcement to a single person. We are special in God's eyes but we are no more special that anyone else. We are probably not the next Moses or Elijah. God can speak through anyone; He even spoke through a donkey (Num. 22:28). If God speaks through us, it is because God chose to do so. It is not because we are particularly special.

Chapter 8: The Worship & Praise Prayer

God responds to those who worship and praise Him. God seeks our worship and praise.

> *But the time is coming—indeed it's here now—when true worshipers will worship the Father in spirit and in truth. The Father is looking for those who will worship him that way.*
> *John 4:23 NLT*

We do this in many ways: music, singing, dancing, gratitude, and giving to name a few. We also worship and praise God in and through prayer. One of the essential ingredients in our relationship with Him is worship and praise.

Worship and praise must come from our spirits. Worship and praise should never be something that we do because we are "supposed" to. John 4:23 (above) says that God is looking for worshippers that worship Him in spirit and in truth (from the heart).

The first part of the Lord's Prayer (Matt. 6:9-13) is a prayer of worship and praise. Paul's prayer for the Ephesians (Eph. 3:14-21) both begins and ends in worship and praise. Paul's prayer for the Christians in Rome begins with worship and praise (Rom. 1:8). All of Paul's prayers, and there are many of them, begin, end, or contain prayers of worship and praise for God the Father and for the Lord Jesus Christ Himself.

In the Modern Church, the term "worship" is almost synonymous with "music." We even call the music portion of the service the "Worship Service" and music leader the "Worship Leader." There is nothing wrong with this; but, it can be misleading. Some people may think that music is the only way to worship God. In fact, there are many, many ways to worship God in many, many different forms; music being just one of them. Generosity, helping others, volunteering, tithes & offerings, or fasting can be just as much a form of worship as music.

> **At its core, worship and praise are simply acknowledging <u>to God</u> that He is incredible, amazing and awesome in every possible sense and wanting to know Him better and to be in His presence.**

Worship and praise encompasses things like thanksgiving, gratitude, glory, splendor, and the magnificence of God. The concept of worship and praise indicates that it is ongoing and active. In other words, the majesty of God never becomes commonplace or taken for granted.

As creatures of flesh-and-blood who get caught up in the daily duties of flesh-and-blood life, it can be easy to lose sight of the wondrous God that we have. Perhaps this is why God reminds us in the Scriptures, over-and-over again, of the stories of creation, the parting of the Red Sea, and the promises He made to Abraham. We flesh-and-blood creatures forget! We need to be reminded on a constant basis. Journaling is a good way to recall all of the things that God has done specifically for us.

It takes time to shift gears from the world of taking the kids to soccer practice to the world of spiritual things. A short time of meditation may be appropriate before you begin to pray.

A prayer of worship and praise is a prayer of remembering the things God has done and honoring the wisdom, mercy, and grace that He continually shows us. You will immediately sense His presence and His power when you do this.

The book of Revelation shows us what worship is like in heaven:

Each of the four living creatures had six wings and was covered with eyes all around, even under its wings. Day and night they never stop saying:

"'Holy, holy, holy
is the Lord God Almighty,
who was, and is, and is to come."
Whenever the living creatures give glory, honor and thanks to him who sits on the throne and who lives forever and ever, the twenty-four elders fall down before him who sits on the throne and worship him who lives forever and ever. They lay their crowns before the throne and say:

"You are worthy, our Lord and God,
to receive glory and honor and power,
for you created all things,
and by your will they were created
and have their being."

Revelation 4:8-11 NIV

There is a funny thing about worship and praise. It doesn't matter how low you are. It doesn't matter how much your world is falling apart. It doesn't matter how hopeless your situation is, when you start praising God, it will lift you up out of the quagmire of darkness. It will rejuvenate your soul. It will give you hope when there is none to be found.

Praise in Spiritual warfare

How powerful is praise? In 2 Chronicles chapter 20 we have the story of a battle that took place between the army of Judah under King Jehoshaphat and the combined armies of the Moabites, Ammonites, and some Meunites.   The army of Judah was greatly outnumbered. King Jehoshaphat turned to the Lord in this time of trouble. The LORD told King Jehoshaphat through the prophet Jahaziel:

> *Do not be afraid or discouraged because of this vast army. For the battle is not yours, but God's.*
> *2 Chronicles 20:15b NIV*

When King Jehoshaphat and all the people of Judah heard this, they worshipped the LORD. The next day, Judah prepared for battle; however, King Jehoshaphat did something very odd; something that we as Christians need to learn to do. He placed singers, and instruments, and dancers at the head of the army and they went into a hopeless battle and badly outnumbered, worshipping and praising God.

The LORD gave them victory. He created confusion in the opposing armies and they began killing each other. They completely wiped themselves out. The only thing that the armies of Judah had to do was to worship and praise God! This is how powerful that praise and worship can be.

Remember this story. When we face troubles or insurmountable problems, when all seems lost and hopeless, when the world is collapsing in on us and around us, remember the story of Jehoshaphat and how God responding to his hopeless situation when worship and praise entered into the equation.

Chapter 9: The Thanksgiving Prayer

The prayer of *Thanksgiving* is very similar to the prayer of *Worship and Praise*. The prayer of Thanksgiving is how we feel about what God has done for us. It is often times expressed without words; raw emotion…praying in the Spirit.

The prayer of Worship and Praise is how we feel about God; HIs majesty, His power, His benevolence, His mercy and grace, His awesome presence. It may not be possible to have one without the other.

Remember that our primary purpose as Christians is to honor God. God says that thanksgiving honors Him:

> But giving thanks is a sacrifice that truly honors me. If you keep to my
> path, I will reveal to you the salvation of God.
> Psalm 50:23 NLT

One of surest ways to see God working in our worthless, miserable lives (or in any life for that matter) is to simply start rejoicing and thanking Him for all our circumstances.

> *Rejoice always, pray continually, give thanks in all circumstances; for*
> *this is God's will for you in Christ Jesus.*
> *1 Thessalonians 5:16-18 NIV*

Our situation will begin to change almost immediately. God responds to thanksgiving! Thank Him for your troubles. Praise Him that you are broke and can't pay your bills. Thank Him that your children hate you. Thank Him that disease has rendered parts of your body useless. Thank Him that you are out of work. The point is that we are telling God that we do not understand the calamity that has befallen us. We do not understand how we will ever recover. We do not understand how there is any hope at all; BUT, we know that He is sovereign, He is in control, and He will deliver us into perfect peace (Isaiah 26:3) and abundant life in the here and now (John 10:10).

> I sought the Lord, and he answered me;
>   he delivered me from all my fears.
> Those who look to him are radiant;
>   their faces are never covered with shame.
> This poor man called, and the Lord heard him;
>   he saved him out of all his troubles.
> The angel of the Lord encamps around those who fear him,
>   and he delivers them.
> Psalm 34:4-7 NIV

For this reason, thanksgiving becomes a very powerful tool for opening our lives to the power of God and His ability to change all things into something good (Rom. 8:28). It is also a critical component of effective prayers.

The story of Exodus is an amazing story. It contains many, many lessons and inspirations for us. It reveals a great deal about God and the nature of God. It reveals just how patient He is with us and just how very much He loves us.

One of the lessons of the Exodus story is the story of thanksgiving; or more precisely, the story of the lack of thanksgiving. The Israelites had been Egyptian slaves for 400 years. God released them from slavery to take them to the Promised Land, the land of milk and honey (Ex. 3:17), the land that He had promised to them long ago (Gen. 17:8).

To get to the promised land, the Israelites, numbering about 2 million people, had to cross through the wilderness. At every turn the Israelites grumbled and complained…they often insisted that they be returned to slavery in Egypt.

Finally they arrived at the promised land after having witnessed their release from Egypt, the parting of the Red Sea, the fire on Mount Sinai, the voice of God, the manna, the quail, and the water from the rock. At this juncture, they should have complete trust in God; however, they were afraid of the people living in the Promised Land and did not believe that God could overcome them (Num. 14:2-4). After everything they had seen and witnessed, they did not believe God! Needless to say, God decided that none of these people would ever see the Promised Land (except Joshua and Caleb who did believe). God sent them back into the wilderness for 40 years until all of the complainers and doubters were dead (Num. 14:32-35).

We can learn so much about thanksgiving from this story. We see that thanksgiving and trusting God are linked. One creates the other. <u>We should recognize that God sends all of us into the wilderness, at some point</u>, in order to bring us to a better place. It is how we view God while we are in the wilderness that determines how long we will stay there! If we are thankful and trust that God will deliver us, He will. If we are not, we could wallow in our bitterness and despair for a very long time.

Thanksgiving opens the door to change. It opens the door to the power of God working in our lives. Effective prayer cannot exist without it.

Is your marriage in trouble? Try this: Go into every room of your house and pray a prayer to God thanking Him for every single thing you can think of about your spouse and watch how your marriage changes.

Are you depressed? Sing songs to God and praise and thank Him for everything that you can think of. Your depression will go away.

Are you afraid? Lift up holy hands in prayer and thanksgiving and the supernatural peace of God will fill you.

Are you worried about your son or daughter? Sing praises to your Father in heaven.
Thank Him for giving you this child. Tell Him you are worried. Tell Him you are afraid.
Then thank Him that He is sovereign in all situations and circumstances. Trust Him.

Thanksgiving so powerful that it will demolish satanic strongholds, bring about change
in people's lives, and free those who are trapped in sinful behaviors and addictions.

The prayer of thanksgiving, working in conjunction with trusting in God, will get you out
of the wilderness!

Chapter 10: Praying For Others

Praying for others is pretty broad in scope. The prayer types of healing, supplication, and spiritual warfare can also encompass praying for others. We pray for other people in many ways. It is probably the most common type of prayer in our churches today. Most prayer requests are requests for other people.

I love to pray for other people. It is one of my favorite ways to *love-on someone*. Often times prayer is the only help that we can offer in a situation. As Christians, praying for others should make up a fundamental part of our prayer life.

> *not looking to your own interests but each of you to the interests of the others.*
> *Philippians 2:4 NIV*

Intercessory Prayer

Praying for other people is often called Intercessor Prayer. Intercessory prayer is very different in the Old and New Testaments. In the Old Testament, people needed a mediator between them and God. Priests, Prophets and special people of the Old Testament, like Daniel, took on the responsibility because ordinary people could not enter into the presence of God. Ordinary people did not have the same access to God. When Christ died on the cross, He became the ultimate mediator (Heb. 8:6).

In the New Testament, we can enter into the presence of God (Heb. 4:16). We no longer require special people to pray on our behalf. Old Testament intercessory prayer doesn't exist anymore. We pray for other people simply because we love them, not because of any type of responsibility that we may have. It is based solely upon the love and compassion that we have for them. Our love for them, along with the direction of the Holy Spirit, guides us to share in their pain, to empathize with their worry, to participate in their concern, and so, we reach out to God, the only Source that can bring hope to any situation. We enter into His presence filled with compassion. We learned in chapter 3 that God responds to our compassion for others.

New Testament intercessory prayer, like Old Testament intercessory prayer, is also prayer that is made on behalf of others. Christians, who are a chosen people, a royal priesthood (1 Peter 2:9), and have access to God, pray on behalf of unbelievers and their interests all the time.

Praying For The Salvation of Others

One of the things that we ask from God for other people is that they come to know Christ as their personal Savior. I have heard this prayer. I'm sure you have to. How can God answer this prayer and still give people the free to will to make their own choice? Without getting into the whole doctrine of predestination let me say this:

- I believe that our prayers for the unsaved are heard by God (I Tim. 2:4).
- I believe that God answers those prayers "Yes", 100% of the time provided we are faithful and persistent in making the request (Luke 18:1) though it may take many years and we may not see the results in our lifetime.
- I believe that God answers those prayers by bringing about the times, circumstances, and events in that person's life that opens their eyes to the truth (Gen. 50:20).
- I believe that the Holy Spirit begins to work on that person's heart and mind from the very first prayer (John 16:8).

It is not that God forces this person to become a Christ follower in response to our prayers; but, that God allows events to take place in that person's life that will enable them to see the person, power and love of Jesus Christ in their lives and they freely choose salvation of their own volition. I've seen the most hardened of hearts broken by their circumstances.

The Lake of Fire was prepared for the Devil and his angels (Matt. 25:41). It is God's desire that all men come to salvation (1 Tim. 2:4). God will respond to your prayers for the salvation of others; but, be prepared; it may be a very long road to take.

Praying For Others And The Holy Spirit

When it comes to praying for others, one of the skills that Christians need to learn to develop is that of listening to the Holy Spirit. There are so many prayer requests out there that one could spend their entire life praying for other people. This is not God's design for us. It is very important to understand what I am about to say:

God gives us different tasks and concerns. This includes different people to pray for. <u>To pray effectively, we must be focused on certain things. We can't be focused on everything and everybody and still be effective!</u> When someone makes a prayer request, we probably should not accept the responsibility of praying for that request unless the Holy Spirit guides us to do so. Spend some time seeking direction from God before you take on the role of praying for a prayer request.

Answered prayer requires compassion and concern for that prayer request. If the Holy Spirit has not touched your heart by giving you compassion for that situation, your prayers will be nothing more than words. But, if the Holy Spirit has touched your heart, then you need to be in earnest prayer for that person and their situation. You are one of the ones that God has chosen to be faithful in prayer for this situation. This is almost certainly an indication that God is about to do something amazing.

I cannot emphasize this enough. <u>God doesn't give you every problem in the world as your personal charge. Listen to the Holy Spirit. Take responsibility only for those things that He puts on your heart. The other things are not yours.</u> They belong to someone else. The things that the Holy Spirit has put on your heart should be pursued with fervor and diligence, lifting this up in prayer daily until the Lord has dealt with the situation in some way.

This prayer concept does not necessarily apply to *one-time prayers*. It applies to *prayer campaigns*. A one-time prayer might be the prayer that you say before you go on a trip, eat a meal, or start a job. A prayer campaign is committing to pray for a prayer request on a daily or regular basis.

Praying For Our Enemies

Jesus told us to love our enemies and pray for those who persecute you (Matt. 5:44). The Greek word for enemies is, ***echthros,*** which means anyone who is openly hostile to us. Often times in prayer meetings I hear people request prayer for a bad situation at work, a bad situation with a neighbor, or a bad situation within the family where an openly hostile person is creating problems. They bring the problem before the prayer meeting so that we will ask God to resolve the situation.

In these situations, I ask the person if they have prayed for this troublemaker; not about the situation, but, "<u>Have you prayed for this troublemaker?</u>" Invariably the answer is usually that they have not. There are no coincidences in the life of a Believer. God gives us challenges so that we might grow and develop. If you are not looking and expecting this type of thing from God, then you might miss it and you might miss the lesson. If you miss it, guess what, God will revisit this lesson with you, at another time, until you learn to respond correctly.

If we are not praying for this troublemaker, then God is probably revealing to us a lack-of-love problem in our own lives. Taking our "lack-of-love-problem" with our enemy to our prayer meeting so that we can circumnavigate the love problem is not a good way to handle this. This problem indicates that God is revealing our heart. The correct thing to do is to privately approach God and pray for this troublemaker (Matt. 5:44). Ask God to give us a spirit of love for this person. When this change happens in our heart, we will find that, in most cases, this former troublemaker will either become our best friend or will be removed from our presence within a week or two of our attitude change. It is astounding how this works.

The troublemaker was placed in our life to reveal a heart problem in our life. These things just don't happen out of the blue. They are planned. If we respond badly, the problem will eventually go away only to return in the form of another troublemaker down the road.

This is true not only with troublemakers, but also with money management, relationships, intimacy, careers, investing, budgeting, etc. If we fail to learn the lesson that God is teaching us, we are doomed to return to the problem at a later date.

Chapter 11: Petition and Supplication

do not be anxious about anything, but in everything by prayer and supplication with thanksgiving let your requests be made known to God.
Philippians 4:6 ESV

A good definition of the prayer of petition or supplication would be "a humble request made for something desired either for yourself or on behalf of someone else." Like praying for others, this type of prayer is common in prayer meetings and public prayers. It is difficult to find the line (if there is one) between them. Examples of this type of prayer might be:

- Asking God to provide a new job for your unemployed neighbor
- Praying that God will provide you will a new car because your old one is breaking down on a regular basis.
- Asking God to provide school supplies for your child because you don't have the money.
- Asking God to find you a babysitter.
- Praying that God will create a certain opportunity for you.
- Asking God to give you a specific gift or talent.

Things! In the prayer of petition/supplication we are generally asking God for things. Christians sometimes have a problem with this unless they are asking for things for the needy. Most Christians are reluctant to ask God for things for themselves. We see this as selfish.

Go back to your children, parents or friends again. Your 7 year old child is about to have his 8th birthday and he is asking you for the new X-5 Super Ray Blaster. Does your child need the new X-5 Super Ray Blaster? Probably not. Yet, for his birthday, he opens his presents to find not only the new X-5 Super Ray Blaster, but all of the accessories, batteries, cords and cables that go along with it! Imagine that! Do you think that God is any different when it comes to His own dear children?

I'm not one to pray for something for me that is unnecessary; but, occasionally I do. I ask God for the minimum level of my desire as a means to assuage my guilt for asking for an unnecessary thing. It always amazes me that God will not only provide my minimum desire, but then He showers me with far more than I ever dreamed or asked for. I am reminded of Malachi 3:10:

> *Bring the whole tithe into the storehouse, that there may be food in my*
> *house. Test me in this," says the Lord Almighty, "and see if I will not*
> *throw open the floodgates of heaven and pour out so much*
> *blessing that there will not be room enough to store it.*
> *Malachi 3:10 NIV*

I have felt like this many times. The point is that when the Lord chooses to show us His favor or chooses to bless us, He has a tendency to shower us in a down pour of goodness and blessing; sometimes that blessing is physical as well as spiritual. God has a tendency to provide bigger, better, or in excess to what we ask Him for whether they be needs or wants.

The Kingdom of God

Being a Christian is not about what we can get from God. The Kingdom of God takes place mostly in the spiritual realm. Our treasures are in the spiritual realm (Matt. 6:20). Our hope is in the spiritual realm (Psalm 33:20). Our struggle is in the spiritual realm (Eph. 6:12).

On the other hand, God has a plan for our lives; a plan that serves Him (Jeremiah 29:11). To accomplish His plan, we need resources: time, opportunities, finances, logistics and things. Sometimes we have to ask Him for some of these things. Sometimes these things will be boats, cars, church vans, pavement, bread, financing, workers, buildings, etc. Additionally, while we are attending to the mission that God has designed for us, there are many needs at home that must be met as well. God provides for those too!

The point is that in order to fulfill the plan that God has designed for our life, we need resources. Often times we have to pray for these resources. These resources are nothing more than tools; tools that enable us to serve God according to the design He has created for us.

It helps a great deal to see all things as belonging to God (Ps. 24:1) and all the things that God gives us as merely tools to help others and to accomplish God's plan for our lives. When we start to think of things as belonging to us, then we start to go down the path of greed and coveting.

For example, Money is a grievous subject for most Christians. It is usually because we think in terms of it belonging to us. It actually belongs to God…all of it. God wants us to be responsible with the money He has given us(Pr. 21:20), and God also wants us to be generous with our money (1 Peter 4:10). Money is nothing more than a tool. When we think of money as a tool, we will have plenty of it. When we start to think of money in terms of possessing it, we start to horde it.

James condemns Christians for praying to God for worldly gain (James 4:3). There is nothing wrong with owning a nice car, possessing it with gratitude and thanksgiving. There is plenty wrong with owning a nice car to boast or show off to others how good you are or how successful you are.

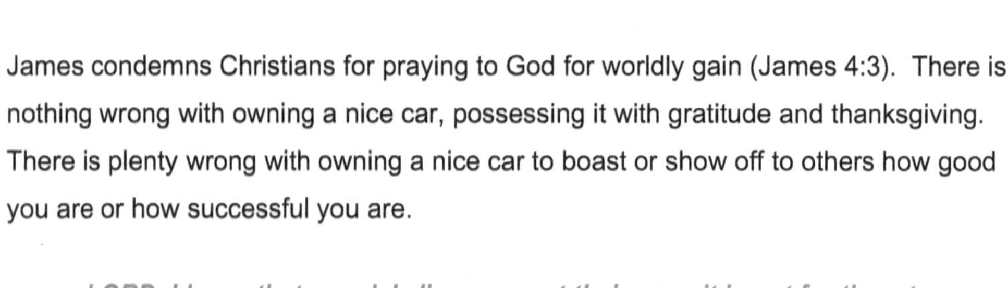

> *LORD, I know that people's lives are not their own; it is not for them to direct their steps.*
> *Jeremiah 10:23 NIV*

It is more about the heart than the prayer request. Your relationship with God will shape your heart so that it conforms to His will.

> *Take delight in the LORD, and he will give you the desires of your heart.*
> *Psalm 37:4 NIV*

Chapter 13: Praying For Healing

Before you read this chapter, you should know that before I write a single word in any of my books, I pray and ask the Holy Spirit to lead me into truth. I really do not want to teach anything that is not from God. In the process, the Holy Spirit teaches me a great deal. Often times the words will flow onto the page almost as if I am an observer.

When I got to this chapter of this book, for 4 days I could not write a word. It was not writers-block because I could go to other chapters and work on them. The problem was with this chapter only. For several years the Holy Spirit has been teaching me about healing and I've been rejecting the teaching as too radical. I would ask myself, "How could mainstream doctrine have missed this?" I was writing this chapter using mainstream theology about healing when the Holy Spirit stopped me cold. I've been doing this long enough to know that when the Holy Spirit stops us on something, it is because we are probably going down the wrong path. I prayed, buried myself in the word, and listened.

At the end of the 4th day, the Holy Spirit let loose the floodgates. Everything I had ever learned about healing simply was not true. In the writing of this chapter, my concept of healing was completely transformed. I prayed, I researched, I translated. This chapter is the result.

Before you read this chapter, I would like to ask that you stop and pray and ask the Holy Spirit to open your mind and guide your thoughts and understanding of this chapter. Repeat my research and see if you don't reach the same conclusions that I did.

Does God heal people today? He certainly does! It happens more often than we are told; especially in the mission field. It could happen more often than it does. The teaching of healing, in the church, is all over the place. It has a tendency to either be abused or ignored.

Healing is alive and well today. Unfortunately, so many churches have gotten caught up in doing things in the flesh that they no longer practice, have knowledge of, or seek the miraculous healing of God.

There are essentially three camps: one says that the Lord will heal everybody provided they have enough faith. Camp two says that says that doctors do God's healing today and miraculous healing is something that we can only hope that the Lord will provide. Camp three believes that God heals people provided it is part of the mysterious will of God. Let's look at the three camps more closely:

Camp One – Healing Through Faith

I don't know who started this absurd idea that if you have enough faith, you will be healed. It has damaged the lives of countless people in the church. There are variations on this such as "if we pray hard enough", "if we fast and pray", "if we quote the word of God", etc.

It doesn't take a great deal of faith to be healed. Jesus healed hundreds, perhaps thousands of people. The 70/72 healed people. The Apostles healed people. I am quite sure that these people were not healed because of their great faith. They were healed because of the power and authority of Jesus Christ!

The only people who could not be healed were the people in Jesus' home town of Nazareth and this is because these people had no faith at all (Matt. 13:58).

Faith is not something that one acquires. Faith is a gift from God (Eph. 2:8-9). There are people that have a great deal of faith, people that have little faith, and people that have a moderate amount of faith. These levels of faith are all a gift from God. They didn't earn it. They didn't deserve it. It was a gift. The idea that you can be worthy of more faith than you have is a works-based theology; it is not from God.

This is not to say that faith cannot grow. It does. If we devote our lives to God and to following His will for our lives, our faith will certainly grow. This is not a reward for faithful service; this is the outcome of watching God work in and through our lives, of watching Him prove His faithfulness time and time again, and of spending time in the presence of holiness (prayer).

Faith can also grow through fasting and prayer. Fasting and prayer puts us into the realm of God. We can see Him more clearly. We can see Him working in our lives and other people's lives more clearly. This action can increase our faith.

We can also pray and ask God to give us more faith; however, it is not the quantity of our faith that matters, it is the object of our faith that gets things done (Luke 17:6).

Camp Two – Doctors and Hope

It is really sad that many Bible believing churches today no longer believe in or seek out miraculous healing from God. Medical science has come a long way since the days of Jesus. Our understanding of disease, infection, healing, and technology borders on the edge of miraculous. The compassion of many of the physicians and medical caregivers is Christ-like in many regards. Despite these advances, we are still in need of miraculous healing from Jesus. The church has either forgotten this or does not believe in the healing power of Jesus.

Doctors treat pain and suffering. Their objective deals with restoring the physical body to its normal a state; at least to as normal as possible.   Jesus also treated pain and suffering. His objective; however, was (is) to bring the soul to life (John 3:3) and to bring glory to God (John 11:4).

If physical healing was Jesus' objective, He could have waved His arm across the whole crowd and healed everybody with the wave of His arm. He did not do this. He chose instead to interact personally with everyone He healed; one-on-one.

Jesus used healing as a tool to teach people the Gospel, and to show people here on earth that He had authority over sickness and that He is the Son of God (Mark 2:1-12). This tool is just as valid and necessary today as it was during the time of Jesus.

Camp Three – Willers

Within the Fundamentalist camp there is the belief that God can heal any disease; however, only if it is the will of God. This is vaguely true; however, it is putting the cart before the horse. It comes from worshipping God in the flesh, not in the spirit.

Willers have no idea who the Holy Spirit is or how to listen to Him. Healing takes place because the Holy Spirit speaks to a Believer and tells them to heal this person in the name of Jesus Christ. This takes place either through prayer, laying of hands, or taking authority over the disease in the name of Jesus.

> **God's will is known before we pray for healing.**

While Jesus is always the source of healing, He can heal through doctors, the laying on of hands, or by miraculous healing.

The Structure of Healing in the New Testament

One of the problems with healing prayers is that we have virtually no examples of it in the New Testament. Jesus healed many, many people; but, Jesus had authority over sickness and disease and He used that authority to heal. He never prayed before He healed someone. He healed them simply by taking authority over the sickness, disease, or malady and healed the person.

The authority was so strong that people who touched Him were healed (Matt. 14:36).

When Jesus sent out the 12 (Mark 6:7-13) and the 70/72 (Luke 10:1-23), He gave them authority to heal as well. When Peter and John healed the lame man they did so using the authority of Jesus (Acts 3:6), not prayer. Peter healed everyone who was brought to him (Acts 5:15-16). It was not through prayer but by taking authority over the condition in the name of Jesus Christ. Paul healed many, even raised them from the dead (Acts 20:10). Only once was there prayer (Acts 28:8) for healing. It was always the Christian (in the name of Jesus) or Jesus Himself taking authority over the disease or condition.

Let Us Take This Up One Notch

In almost every instance mentioned above where authority was exercised over disease, authority was also given over demons and demonic influence. In the New Testament, there is a close connection between some sicknesses and conditions and demonic influence.

In the modern church; especially the churches who are not Spirit filled, the concept of demons and demonic activity being associated with disease is rejected (though many of these churches believe in demons and demonic activity, just not in association with illness). The idea is attributed to medically ignorant people, during the time of Jesus, who assign unknown medical conditions to demons. The New Testament account of the mute boy with an unclean spirit (Mark 9:14-29) specifically attributes the condition to a demon. Jesus did not heal the boy, He cast out the demon. The account in Mark 9 does sound a lot like epilepsy; however, the New Testament recognizes a difference between epilepsy and demon possession:

> *News about him spread as far as Syria, and people soon began bringing to him all who were sick. And whatever their sickness or disease, or if they were demon possessed or epileptic or paralyzed—he healed them all.*
> *Matthew 4:24 NLT*

If this story is not true because of medically ignorant people calling a disease, demon possession, then we have a fundamental problem. What other stories in the Bible are not true because of ignorance? We can't pick and choose which parts of the Bible are from God and which parts of the Bible are due to ignorance. We have to believe either that the whole Bible is the inspired word of God or that none of it is. The same is true for healing, sickness and demonic involvement.

Peter told Cornelius about Jesus and described Him like this:

> *how God anointed Jesus of Nazareth with the Holy Spirit and power, and how he went around doing good and healing all who were under the power of the devil, because God was with him.*
> *Acts 10:38 NIV*

The link between demonic activity and illness is too pronounced in the New Testament to be ignored in our walk with God. Is there any reason to believe that the close connection between some sicknesses and demonic influence still exist today? Of course it still exists. The Bible says that demons are involved in some illness and therefore, we must be aware of this in our healing activities. In today's world, there is a profusion of new diseases and disorders that did not exist in New Testament times; especially mental disorders. There is also a profusion of socially acceptable sin. When it comes to sickness, everyone is looking for healing. Perhaps, at least in some instances, we should be looking for demons instead!

Sickness is Complex

Sickness, disease, and maladies are complex in the spiritual context. Sometimes these things have their roots in demonic activity; but, there are many other factors. Sin is the leading cause of sickness; not as in God's punishment for sin; but, as in reaping the harvest of the seeds we have sown.

Excessive cigarette smoking causes lung cancer, emphysema, and numerous other diseases. Drinking excessive alcohol leads to cirrhosis, immune disorders, and nerve disorders.   Having unprotected sex with multiple partners leads to HIV and other sexually transmitted diseases. Excessive drug use leads to rotten teeth, inability to cope, and depression. Eating too much makes you overweight. Being overweight leads to heart disease, diabetes, high blood pressure, joint and back pain, and other maladies.

The age of electronics has opened a Pandora's box of new disorders. We become addicted to watching television, to surfing the Internet, to checking our phones, to checking our watches. We are addicted to video games, chat rooms, texting, social networking, internet porn, and child porn. Children have taken innocent emojis and formed a whole new language where they can buy drugs, have sex, and make plans all the while deceiving their parents in every way.

Laziness, pride and arrogance, greed, lust, lying, and indifference are becoming the norm in our society and, left unchecked, they all lead to sickness in one form or another.

Our lifestyles create enormous amounts of stress in our lives. According to the Mayo Clinic and many other researchers, stress increases sickness and disease.

90% or more of all of our problems are created by our own doing. Is it fitting to ask God for healing when our sickness is the result of our own foolishness and disobedience? The short answer is *YES* because when God found us and redeemed us, we were pretty worthless then too. By His incomprehensible mercy and grace He saved us anyway. We have never been worthy of the blood of Christ. We have never been worthy of redemption. What's more, Christ died for us, long before we were born, knowing what we would be and the things we would do; still, He gave His life for us (Romans 5:8). Praise be to God that He does not abandon us in the deep, dark pool of our own foolishness!

> *All praise to God, the Father of our Lord Jesus Christ. It is by his great mercy that we have been born again, because God raised Jesus Christ from the dead. Now we live with great expectation,*
> *1 Peter 1:3 NLT*

The complexity of healing becomes even more complicated when we throw in the fact that we live in a fallen world. While God has the ability to cure our cancer, or to heal our broken leg, or to stop our aging process, sickness, disease and entropy are attributes of a fallen world. Sooner or later, our bodies will die. Healing is not something that we can demand from God. Yet, sometimes, God wishes to show His sovereignty over sickness and disease by allowing healing. Sometimes God works healing through doctors. Sometimes He works healing through spiritual gifts. Sometimes He works healing through prayers. However healing might come, it is not an "on demand" miracle service available to those who believe.

Sometimes, God does not heal. Healing is not a works-based event so the idea that healing did not take place has nothing do with how good person you are or how good a person the person who prayed for you is. The trigger, the defining essence of healing can only come from the Holy Spirit speaking directly to us.

Healing And The Book of James

In the 5th chapter of the book of James (vs.13-19) we have, what is generally considered to be, the definitive source of healing in the New Testament. The only problem is that it is not the definitive source of healing in the New Testament!

We are taught that if someone in the church is sick, we should take them before the Elders of the church. The Elders will anoint them with oil in the name of Jesus and pray over them and they will be healed.   James was awfully vague in his instruction when he wrote this letter to the 12 tribes scattered among the nations. When you look at different translations, there is good deal of difference. In other words, it is not all that definitive.

I've been studying the Bible long enough to know that when you encounter vagueness in the Bible, it is usually because there was difficulty in the translating.   I'm no Greek scholar; but, I would put my self-taught Greek up against anyone who has studied Greek with no shame or remorse. I decided to translate James 5:13-19, word-for-word, from the original Greek to find out exactly what was going on. Don't worry, I'm not going to bore you by getting into the technical aspects of this research; but, I will share the things I learned.

The sickness addressed by James is not illness or disease. It is being exhausted to the point of sickness due to overwork and/or sin. It is brokenness ! The healing for which the Elders of the church (Greek: Any mature Christian) are being called, is healing from the power of sin; not necessarily illness or disease; addiction would be a better culprit. Then verse 16, confess your sins…so that you might be healed. Verse 19, if you should wander from the truth…and be brought back. Finally, James concludes the section by saying:

Healing

I think that if you put together all the pieces that have been given to us in the New Testament that God would prefer that we obtain miraculous healing by taking authority over the illness in the name of Jesus Christ. <u>It's not that praying for healing is wrong, it is that taking authority over the condition, in the name of Jesus, is better.</u>

It is like this: to support the spreading of the Gospel, some of us write a check to support missions work in some foreign land; distant, remote, detached; yet, still doing good. There is really nothing wrong with this; however, God would prefer that we participate directly by talking to the guy next door first. It is far more intimate, complete, and involved. When there are results, it is far more rewarding.

Healing is a lot like that. The healing prayer is distant, remote, detached; yet, still doing good. Taking authority over the illness, in the name of Jesus, is far more intimate, complete, and involved. When there are results, it is far more rewarding.

So, should we go around and just start healing people? Absolutely not! Healing still belongs to the will of God and God's plan; otherwise, we would have a bunch of 2000 year old Christians running around the planet. We should never try to heal someone unless we are prompted by the Holy Spirit to do so; this includes praying for someone to be healed. It is our daily surrender to the Holy Spirit that enable us to hear His voice and then know what to do.

When you do feel the prompting of the Holy Spirit, try to find one or two other people who are like you to go with you. In Matthew 18:15-20, we have verse 20:

> *For where two or three gather in my name, there am I with them.*
> *Matthew 18:20 NIV*

This verse is often misused by Christians to indicate that God is present when two or more gather together in His name. The corollary to this idea would be that whenever one person is present that Christ is not present. We know that the corollary is not true so this verse is taken out of context.

The context of Matthew 18:15-20 is dealing with discipline in the church and that when taking disciplinary action in the church, two or three should agree and that when they do, the authority of Christ will be with them.

> *Truly I tell you, whatever you bind on earth will be bound in heaven, and*
> *whatever you loose on earth will be loosed in heaven. "Again, truly I tell*
> *you that if two of you on earth agree about anything they ask for, it will*
> *be done for them by my Father in heaven. For where two or three gather*
> *in my name, there am I with them."*

Church discipline requires the authority of Christ. Healing also requires the authority of Christ. In these verses, we have the perfect model for all activities that require the authority of Christ; including taking authority over sickness.

If the person being healed is someone close to you, it is very easy to confuse God's will with your own will. Having another person or two, who listens to the Holy Spirit, with you will help you to discern God's will in your situation. Also, having another person or two with you will guide you in discerning whether you are taking authority over sickness or taking authority over demonic activity.

If the Holy Spirit is prompting you and you are unable to find others that agree with you or unable to get them there in a prompt manner, do what the Holy Spirit is telling you to do anyway. Waiting or postponing what the Spirit is telling you to do is quenching the Spirit. Something we are told not to do (1 Thess. 5:19).

If the Holy Spirit prompts you and/or your group and you take authority over the disease in the name of Jesus, that person will be healed! The transformation is instantaneous. It is not "down the road" or "God has started the healing process". It will happen then and there. If the Holy Spirit prompts you and/or your group to pray instead, then that person will be healed; but, the transformation may happen down the road or in an unexpected way. This is why listening to the Holy Spirit is the trigger.

Never forget that it was God who healed the person; not you. God gave all Christians this ability. This authority is not one of the gifts of healing; this authority is a responsibility that all Christians have to use over the power of Satan in our lives. This applies not only to healing, but to all types of spiritual warfare.

The Healing Prayer

In the story of the demon possessed boy that we discussed in Mark 9, we not only have Jesus healing the boy by casting out a demon, but, we also have glimpses of healing prayer. The disciples, who had authority to heal and to cast out demons, could not heal or cast out the demon from this boy. When they asked Jesus about it, Jesus said that this type of demon can only come out by prayer (some manuscripts have prayer and fasting) (Mark 9:29).

We also have a glimpse of the healing prayer in Acts 28 where Paul, while shipwrecked on the island of Malta, went to the estate of Publius, the chief official of the island. Publius' father was sick with fever and dysentery. Paul prayed and then laid hands on the father and the father was healed (vs. 8). We don't know if Paul was praying for healing or if he was just praying. We have no details of the prayer or its purpose.

While taking authority over sickness in the name of Jesus seems to be God's preferred method of healing, this applies only to when God's will is known via the Holy Spirit. Sometimes the Holy Spirit doesn't move us in the direction of the spontaneous miracle. Sometimes He moves in the direction of prayer. While I cannot document this specific situation in the New Testament by example, we can presuppose this as true by the by the broad applications that we have for prayer:

… to cite just a few

It may be that the time is not right for healing to take place. It may be that God wants to use another person to initiate healing. Perhaps God is using the situation to bring about brokenness. It may be that God is going to heal through doctors. It may be that God wants to use this situation for another purpose. It may be that we have never learned to listen to the Spirit of God. When God doesn't speak, all we can do is to pray and wait (Ps. 46:10) and trust in the Lord (Is. 12:2).

In reality, <u>I am certain that a great deal more healing would be taking place if only more Christians were walking in the Spirit and expecting God to do miraculous things. This applies not only to healing, but with all the things that we pray for.</u> We default to the healing prayer either due to ignorance or because it does not require the level of commitment that walking in Spirit requires.

This does not mean that the healing prayer is weak. On the contrary, the healing prayer is very powerful. I am witness to its power and on many occasions I have seen God heal people through prayer alone. The healing prayer is usually less dramatic and slower than taking authority in the name of Jesus Christ; but, it is still effective.

My Experience With The Healing Prayer

I do not have one of the spiritual gifts for healing. My spiritual gifts are discernment (the supernatural ability to distinguish, judge, or appraise a person's statement, situation, or environment) and exhortation (the supernatural ability to encourage, strengthen, or motivate others). Nevertheless, I have been richly blessed by God as having taken part in miraculous healing from healing prayer on several occasions. Most of my experience took place before I developed prayer skills or understood taking authority over disease in the name of Jesus.

Let me begin by reminding you what I said back in chapter 3:

> **God puts certain events and people on our hearts and these are the things we should be praying for... It is simply not possible to have compassion or empathy for every single problem on the planet.**

We have to remember this! <u>Don't pray for things that God has not put on your heart! Without genuine, Holy Spirit infused compassion, we are just mouthing the words</u>. This includes healing. Most prayer meetings diverge in to mostly prayers for healing that are prayed from a list. I have taken part in many such meetings. I have prayed for the healing of people because I was assigned to pray for them, feeling nothing the process.

There have been other times; however, when the Spirit of God grabbed me and assigned a situation to ME! The Holy Spirit fills me with compassion and empathy for the person(s) and the family. When this happens, I cannot stop praying for the situation. Most of the time, I am prompted to lay hands on the person. When the Holy Spirit gets a hold of me like this, 100% of the time the person is healed. I might also add that there are others also praying for this person(s). It might be instantaneous or at

some point in the very near future. Sometimes it is miraculous – out of nowhere.
Sometimes it is miraculous – through a doctor. In every case; however, the person is
healed and no one knows exactly what happened.

There was an odd case that happened in a church that I used to attend. There was a
devout Christian woman that got very sick. The church had gone through about 12
years of pastors who had personal agendas rather than a Holy Spirit agenda. The
church was broken and had lost about half of its' congregation. The congregation loved
the Lord but they were caught up in the New Legalism and had not seen God work in
their church for many years. It was about this time that I came to the church with a
message of God's grace and of a big God who answers prayer. I received lots of push-
back.

The church began to pray for the sick woman; however, there was not a coordinated
effort to do so. It was kind of a haphazard, hodge-podge of hope and wishing. The
worst part was that the church was full of Willers. The Pastor, the Elders and even the
sick woman and her husband were Willers.

If there ever was time that this church needed to see God work, it was now. Here was
the perfect opportunity for the church to see a big God. Here was the perfect
opportunity for the church to experience revival and rejuvenation. Out of the blue I was
filled with the Holy Spirit and He was telling me to lay hands on the woman and pray for
her in public. Oddly enough, my two best friends and prayer partners experienced the
very same direction from the Holy Spirit separately and independently. We had three
Spirit filled Christians being directed by the Holy Spirit to lay hands on the sick woman
and pray for her in public.

When we reached out to the woman for the opportunity to pray for her, she was
surrounded by a wall of Willers. No visitors! Pray for her at home! We were denied the

opportunity. These Willers are Christians. I'm sure that I will see most of them in heaven; however, Satan had such influence over them that they were doing his bidding just as Peter did Satan's bidding in front of Jesus:

> *Jesus turned and said to Peter, "Get behind me, Satan! You are a stumbling block to me; you do not have in mind the concerns of God, but merely human concerns."*
> *Matthew 16:23 NIV*

The woman's condition continued to get worse until she finally died. Never have I been more certain of God wanting to heal someone. Never have I been more certain that God wanted to reveal His power and presence to a congregation; but, the congregation was never in union and the Willers created so much doubt that they never believed that God was going to heal her. So God had nothing to work with.

My friends and I prayed for the woman from afar; however, this was not what God wanted. He wanted the congregation to know that a group of people laid hands on and prayed for the woman and that she was healed by the power of God. He wanted the congregation to know that they worshipped a big God who created all things and is able to do all things. God was willing to rejuvenate the congregation, but they refused to believe in His power, strength, and His love for them.

> *And so he did only a few miracles there because of their unbelief.*
> *Matthew 13:58 NLT*

This event affected me a great deal. It was the first time that I became aware of the power of unbelief. The doubt created by the Willers, wolves in sheep's clothing and emissaries of Satan, in the church and oh how destructive they are. They would rather let a person die than to take a chance of witnessing the actual power and glory of the God they supposedly worship.

Suppose we were wrong. Suppose that we were just charismatic nutzoids. What harm would it have done to pray for her? On the other hand, what if we were right? What a glorious thing we all would have witnessed! The woman would be with us today and God would be glorified. The Willers chose to give the miraculous no opportunity at all. The Willers chose to give no opportunity at all for God to be glorified which, by the way, happens to be the very same mission of Satan.

So How Do We Pray For Healing?

If the Holy Spirit has directed us to pray for the healing of someone, then we should pray. We should begin the healing prayer with the fellowship prayer where we spend time with the Father trying to seek His will for this situation. If He reveals to us His will, then pray for that. If He doesn't reveal His will to us, then we should pray as the Spirit leads us. We should pray as often as the Holy Spirit leads us. Pray for complete recovery, or pray for the doctors to heal. or pray for miraculous healing, etc. Pick a direction. Pick an outcome. Once you are in motion, the Lord will guide in the direction that you should be praying.

Remember the qualities of prayers that get answered from chapter 3. Remember that the primary reason we are here is bring glory to God (Isaiah 43:7). Our prayers and our prayer requests should bring glory and honor to God. Our prayer requests should cause others to worship and praise God (Matt. 5:16). This means, as a general rule, that we should involve others in our healing prayer, either through joint praying or by making it known that we are praying. This is so that when the healing takes place, others will know that it was God and they will participate in our worship and praise.

Avoid secret prayers for healing.

Chapter 14: Prayer and Spiritual Warfare

Spiritual warfare is mostly dismissed in the modern church. Even churches that believe in Satan, demons, and hell, put very little teaching, preaching, or effort into spiritual warfare.

Satan – The Devil

The devil is real. He is very real. He is often seen as a cute guy in a red suit or as a hideous creature that sucks blood and eats human flesh. In actuality, Satan is incredibly beautiful, incredibly wise, intelligent, alluring, and charismatic. He is also incredibly powerful. He is the most powerful being that God has ever created. He was the head of all the angels in heaven (Ezek. 28:1-19).

Satan is known as the commander of the powers of the unseen world (Eph. 2:2). The antichrist will be the personification of Satan. The antichrist will be smooth, charismatic, brilliant, and wise. He will be a skilled negotiator. He will have the ability to solve all the world's problems (or seemingly so). He will solve the middle east crisis and enable the Israelis to rebuild their temple. He will deceive the whole world. The attributes of the antichrist are the attributes of Satan.

Satan was so powerful, in fact, that he thought he could defeat God (Is.14:13-15). We have a glimpse of his power in this: Satan thought he could defeat God; the same God who spoke everything into existence. For Satan to have thought that, he must be incredibly powerful. When he was cast out of heaven, one third of all the angels in heaven followed Satan and they were cast out of heaven along with him (Rev. 12:4). These fallen angels are known in the Bible as demons. They are agents and emissaries for Satan.

Satan is not omniscient. He does not know our thoughts; however, he reads body language and studies our actions. Satan is not omnipresent; however, because of the number of demons under his control, it would appear that he is omnipresent. We don't know how many demons there are; but, we can be sure there are millions and millions. Hebrews 12:22 says the number of angels is too large to count. This is after one-third have been taken away. We can extrapolate from that description that there are millions and millions of demons.

Satan knows us better than we know ourselves. He and his demon horde know and understand how to bring temptation into our lives. His objective is to rend and wound us; to discourage us and cause us to give up. He wants to create in us bitterness and regret; guilt and shame. He knows what buttons to push. He knows how we have responded to types of events in the past. He knows our weaknesses and our strengths. Additionally he has the power to bring about circumstances, conditions, and events that could put our lives into turmoil, complexity, and distress (Job 1:11).

We learned in the previous chapter that Satan and his angels are involved with some sickness and some physical afflictions. We know that Satan and his demons are seeking to destroy all Christians by seeking to create fear, doubt, despair, depression, anxiety, hatred, unbelief, addiction, lust, greed, perversion, and unfaithfulness (Rev. 12:17). Peter tells us:

> *Stay alert! Watch out for your great enemy, the devil. He prowls around*
> *like a roaring lion, looking for someone to devour.*
> *I Peter 5:8 NLT*

Jesus defeated Satan. The reason that Christ came was to destroy the works of the devil (1 John 3:8). From the temptations in the wilderness to His death on the cross and resurrection, Jesus defeated Satan at every turn. The resurrection was the final defeat

(Col. 2:15) taking away the power of death for those who believe in the power of His name (John 12:31). Amen.

Christians are constantly under attack by Satan and/or his demons. Satan has power over Christians only if we allow him to have it. He is constantly looking for a way to destroy our lives, destroy our marriages, destroy our faith, destroy our families, and to destroy our doctrine. This is why Peter is warning us, "Watch out, stay alert." When we are tempted with fear, doubt, despair, depression, anxiety, hatred, unbelief, addiction, lust, greed, perversion, or unfaithfulness and we give in, we are giving Satan and his demon hordes access to our lives. The Bible says:

> *Submit yourselves, then, to God. Resist the devil, and he will flee from you.*
> *James 4:7 NIV*

When we think of temptation, most of us think of obvious temptations. Things like lust, greed, and debauchery creep into our thoughts. Satan certainly utilizes these tools; however, these things are usually the end and not the means. Typically he is a lot more clever than that. It starts softly and subtlety in the form of a gentle suggestion or a negative thought. If we allow this thought to take root in our minds, then it will begin to grow and blossom into sin.

> *but each person is tempted when they are dragged away by their own evil desire and enticed. Then, after desire has conceived, it gives birth to sin; and sin, when it is full-grown, gives birth to death.*
> *James 1:14-15 NIV*

Spiritual warfare begins with the battle against the small things. Doubt, feelings of worthlessness, feelings of failure, anxiety, depression, guilt, hatred, fear, loneliness, pride, arrogance, etc. are tools of Satan. None of these feelings are from God. To give in to these feelings is to give Satan a foothold in your life. He uses these feelings to plant the seeds of destruction into your life.

Some days, those seeds of destruction are falling all around us. As Christians, we can claim the victory in the name of Jesus Christ. When we see that we are under spiritual attack, we can claim the authority that Jesus has over the devil and we can rebuke the devil in the name of Jesus.

Jesus fought the devil by using scripture when He was tempted in the wilderness (Matt. 4:1-11). Jesus fought the devil by rebuking his demons directly at the exorcism of the Gerasene demoniac (Matt. 8:28-34) and many other exorcisms. Michael, the archangel, fought the devil by using the authority of the Lord to retrieve the body of Moses (Jude 1:9). The angel resisting the demon of the Persian kingdom enlisted the help of the angel Michael to fight against Satan's power (Dan. 10:13). While it is not within our purview to call for the assistance of angels, we know that angels have been sent by God to help us in our fight (Ps. 34:7). In Ephesians chapter 6, Paul gives us additional tools: truth, righteousness, preparedness, faith, salvation, the word of God, and praying in the Spirit.

The Spiritual Realm

The spiritual world is real. It is very real. There is war in heaven. It is the war between the will of God and the will of Satan. The war encompasses the angels in heaven and the demon horde of Satan. It includes the godly man and the ungodly man. Paul says:

> *For our struggle is not against flesh and blood, but against the rulers,*
> *against the authorities, against the powers of this dark world and*
> *against the spiritual forces of evil in the heavenly realms.*
> *Ephesians 6:12 NIV*

In the spirit realm there are rulers and authorities. There is an interwoven connection between the spiritual realm and the physical realm. Some of the afflictions that we face in the physical realm are the result of much larger disturbances in the spiritual realm (Dan. 10:13). What we see and experience is a mere tip of the iceberg.

Elijah prayed that his servant might see a portion of the armies of God:

> *And Elisha prayed, "Open his eyes, Lord, so that he may see." Then*
> *the Lord opened the servant's eyes, and he looked and saw the hills full*
> *of horses and chariots of fire all around Elisha.*
> *2 Kings 6:17 NIV*

The book of Revelation describes things that have taken place in the past and things that will take place in the future. It also describes these things from different points of view. While the book is revealing God's final attempt to save mankind, His final judgment, the new heavens and the new earth, and the mystery of God's love for us through the lamb of God, we also get a clear glimpse of activities taking place in the spiritual realm. It is clear from the book of Revelation that the things taking place in heaven have profound consequences on earth.

We also know that some things that take place in the physical realm have repercussions in the spiritual realm also; the most profound example is the fall of man in the garden of Eden (Gen. 3). We know that there is rejoicing in heaven when one sinner repents (Luke 15:7).

There are also enigmatic things that we do not understand. The temple of the Lord is an example. It was specified in great detail including exact dimensions (Exodus). The temple and its contents, including the Ark of the Covenant, is a pattern on earth of something in heaven (Heb. 8:4-5). The altars, the courtyard, the oil for the lampstand, the garments, the basin, the anointing oil, etc. are all specified in great detail along with the procedures and ceremonies of the Law.

All of these things indicate an umbilical nature between the physical realm and the spiritual realm. As Christians, we cannot ignore this relationship.

The Battle

As Christians, we are a part of this battle (Eph. 6:12). Much of the trouble in our lives is because we give Satan permission to trouble us (James 1:14-15). Much of the trouble in our lives is because we do not take up the weapons that God has given us to fight the battle.

> *The weapons we fight with are not the weapons of the world. On the contrary, they have divine power to demolish strongholds.*
> *2 Corinthians 10:4 NIV*

When our children, or our friend, or our spouse, or our Uncle Jack become involved with or fall victim to the ravages of sin, this calls for spiritual warfare. It calls for prayer, fasting, reading and using the word of God, praising and worshipping God, and using the authority of Jesus to rebuke the devil. We fight with the tools that God has given us. We don't stand around worrying. We go to battle. We go to war.

When Jesus was tempted in the wilderness, Matthew and Mark record that when the devil finished tempting Jesus that angels came and ministered unto Him (Matt. 4:11 & Mark 1:13). <u>The gospel of Luke, however, adds that the devil left Jesus until a more opportune time (Luke 4:13)</u>. When we use God's tools against Satan, he leaves us; but, it is only temporarily. He will return at a more opportune time. The battle is a daily struggle. It comes to us in the form of temptations, irritable people, bad moods, sickness, disease, depression, etc. These are the flaming arrows of the evil one described by Paul in Ephesians 6:16. If you recognize that you are being attacked with flaming arrows, this is a time to pray, to fast, to read and use the word of God, to praise and worship God, and to rebuke the devil using the authority of Jesus Christ.

Remember, the devil cannot read your mind. To rebuke the devil you must do so by speaking out loud something like this:

Satan, in the name of the Lord Jesus Christ, I command you to flee from me!

You are a child of the living God (Gal. 4:7). You are the alive in Christ (Eph. 2:5). Jesus has been given all authority in heaven and on earth:

> *Then Jesus came to them and said, "All authority in heaven and on earth has been given to me.*
> *Matthew 28:18 NIV*

With such inheritance, when we use the authority of Jesus Christ as children of the living God, we know we have been given power over the rulers, the authorities, the powers of this dark world and against the spiritual forces of evil in the heavenly realms.

> *"Truly I tell you, whatever you bind on earth will be bound in heaven, and whatever you loose on earth will be loosed in heaven.*
> *Matthew 18:18 NIV*

Stay alert! Watch out! This is what spiritual warfare is all about. It is recognizing the works of the devil in our lives or in the lives of others and taking steps to prevent him from developing any type of stronghold. The devil will leave you when you rebuke him with the authority of Christ; however, about the time that you think he is gone for good, he will return to try to rend and wound you again, to discourage you, to crush you.

As Christians, we should always be mindful of the war of that is taking place in heavenly realm.   Satan's attack is relentless. It is important that we ask God to make us aware of the works of the devil in our lives, to resist the devil, and to rebuke the devil in the name of Jesus Christ when we see his works in our lives and in the lives of those we love.

Chapter 15: Bringing It All Together

As Christians, we are part of an incredible plan that God has designed for the world. Our role here is not about retirement, spouses, children, grandchildren, careers, vacations, or any of the things that most of us obsess over. Certainly all of those things are gifts from God and play an integral part in our lives; but, they are not our purpose.

We are children of the LORD God Almighty! We are children of the one true God. We are children of the One who created everything. He has created trillions upon trillions of things; yet, He is so intimate with each of us that He even knows the number of hairs on our head (Luke 12:7).

 We were created to be intimate with Him. When Adam and Eve sinned and separated us from that intimacy, God became flesh in Jesus Christ. Jesus died in our place and became the perfect sacrifice for our sin. Jesus restored our ability to be intimate with God. Ladies and Gentlemen, because of Jesus Christ, we can now have fellowship with the Architect, Author, Designer and Creator of all things.

> Thank God for this gift too wonderful for words!
> 2 Corinthians 9:15 NLT

Prayer is our gateway to intimacy with God. Prayer connects us to the Source: the source of peace, the source of joy, the source of love, the source of holiness. Prayer connects us to the will of God. Prayer connects us to the power and strength of God. Prayer centers and balances our lives. Prayer puts us in the presence of holiness. Prayer enables us to walk in the Spirit and therefore not to satisfy the desires of the flesh (Gal. 5:16).

We can't go to God on an occasional basis and think that we have any kind of relationship with Him. What kind of relationship would we have with our spouse or our children if we interacted with them only on an occasional basis?

It is the Spirit of God that transforms and empowers us. The more we yield to the Spirit of God the more we are transformed and empowered. The prayer of daily surrender is the best way to yield to the Spirit of God. It is the best way to enable God to do great things in our lives and to follow the destiny that we were called to live. Jesus said:

> "I am the vine; you are the branches. If you remain in me and I in you,
> you will bear much fruit; apart from me you can do nothing.
> John 15:5 NIV

The meaning of the Greek word for fruit in John 15:5, *karpos*, indicates deeds, actions, results, profits, gains. Again, not boats and cars and houses but deeds, actions, results, profits and gains for Christ.

I am reminded of a couple and their daughter that I knew in Raleigh. Daughter Wendy wanted to have a ministry for her high school friends so she started inviting her friends over on Monday nights. Dad, Dean, liked to cook so he started cooking dinner for the group. The wife (who I think was named Liz) helped with everything. Each week the group would eat and then do some Bible study.

The Lord blessed this simple act. In a short period of time the group grew from 6-7 young people to over 200 young people. The church that the family attended started paying for the food. From this simple meal…from this simple act…dozens of young people accepted Christ as their personal Savior. Some of the young people went on to become missionaries and to serve God in other ways.

This family simply yielded to what the Holy Spirit was telling them to do. In doing so, they impacted the lives of countless people all over the world and gained a great deal for Christ! None of it was planned. None of it was intentional. It was simply yielding. We have the same Spirit living in us. He is speaking to us. He is guiding us. Are we listening?

Once we have accepted Jesus as our personal Savior, the Holy Spirit comes to live inside of us and wakens our dead spirit so that we can have a relationship with the LORD God Almighty. The Holy Spirit enables and empowers us. This newly born spirit, alive within us, is made pure by the shed blood of Jesus and we are able to enter into the very presence of God and have fellowship with Him. This is what prayer is.

I pray that this book has helped you to discover a whole new life of prayer. I pray that it has taught you to pray with power and boldness, to expect God to answer your prayers, to ask God for big things, and to pray to a very big God.

> Now to him who is able to do immeasurably more than all we ask or imagine, according to his power that is at work within us, to him be glory in the church and in Christ Jesus throughout all generations, forever and ever! Amen.
> Ephesians 3:20-21 NIV

ABOUT THE AUTHOR

Mark Nicholas Brady is one of the 52 grandchildren of Rev. Cledith Hefner, a Pastor for the Christian and Missionary Alliance Church for his whole life. As Mark was growing up, he was required to be in attendance at the church just about any time the church doors were opened. He was born in Ohio, but spent most of his adult life in the Raleigh, North Carolina area.

Over the course of his life, Mark has started and sold dozens of companies. He has served on the Board of Directors of many private companies, is a well known International Real Estate Investor, Investment Banker, Home Builder, and Financial Planner.

While Mark has a passion for investing, banking, and money management, he has an even greater passion for serving our Lord. He loves in-depth Bible studies, taught himself to understand ancient Greek, and loves to spend hours teaching and discussing the Bible with others.

In 2017, he married his wife, Catherine (Cathy) H. Brady. Together they have 4 children and 17 grandchildren. He and his wife attend Newpointe Church in Canton, Ohio.